T0192016

Communications in Computer and Information Science 1273

Commenced Publication in 2007
Founding and Former Series Editors:
Simone Diniz Junqueira Barbosa, Phoebe Chen, Alfredo Cuzzocrea,
Xiaoyong Du, Orhun Kara, Ting Liu, Krishna M. Sivalingam,
Dominik Ślęzak, Takashi Washio, Xiaokang Yang, and Junsong Yuan

Editorial Board Members

Joaquim Filipe ⓘ
Polytechnic Institute of Setúbal, Setúbal, Portugal
Ashish Ghosh
Indian Statistical Institute, Kolkata, India
Igor Kotenko ⓘ
*St. Petersburg Institute for Informatics and Automation of the Russian
Academy of Sciences, St. Petersburg, Russia*
Raquel Oliveira Prates ⓘ
Federal University of Minas Gerais (UFMG), Belo Horizonte, Brazil
Lizhu Zhou
Tsinghua University, Beijing, China

More information about this series at http://www.springer.com/series/7899

Dmitrii Rodionov · Tatiana Kudryavtseva ·
Mohammed Ali Berawi ·
Angi Skhvediani (Eds.)

Innovations in Digital Economy

First International Conference, SPBPU IDE 2019
St. Petersburg, Russia, October 24–25, 2019
Revised Selected Papers

 Springer

Editors
Dmitrii Rodionov ⓘ
Peter the Great St. Petersburg
Polytechnic University
St. Petersburg, Russia

Tatiana Kudryavtseva ⓘ
Peter the Great St. Petersburg
Polytechnic University
St. Petersburg, Russia

Mohammed Ali Berawi
University of Indonesia
Depok, Indonesia

Angi Skhvediani ⓘ
Peter the Great St. Petersburg
Polytechnic University
St. Petersburg, Russia

ISSN 1865-0929   ISSN 1865-0937 (electronic)
Communications in Computer and Information Science
ISBN 978-3-030-60079-2   ISBN 978-3-030-60080-8 (eBook)
https://doi.org/10.1007/978-3-030-60080-8

This Springer imprint is published by the registered company Springer Nature Switzerland AG
The registered company address is: Gewerbestrasse 11, 6330 Cham, Switzerland

Preface

The International Scientific Conference on Innovations in Digital Economy (SPBPU DE 2019) was held at Peter the Great St. Petersburg Polytechnic University, Russia, during October 24–25, 2019.

SPBPU IDE 2019 brought together experts from academia and industry to uncover the challenges and solutions to ensure the digital transformation of economic systems. The objective of the conference was to discuss recent contributions and innovations in the digital economy, as well as their consequences for modern society. This conference disseminated the most recent advances in this field and promoted collaborations to maximize opportunities for innovative solutions. The conference aimed to discuss innovative trends in the digital economy and their effects on the contemporary society. It contributes to sharing some information related to the latest achievements in this sphere, leading to further fruitful cooperation that enhances opportunities in innovative solution development. The main purpose of the conference was to estimate current trends and controversies, while developing the digital society, to forecast changes in a strategic run with allowance for minimizing possible risks.

In total 78 papers were received. 8 of the best selected papers were accepted to be published in this CCIS post-proceedings volume. All submitted papers passed a three-stage review process. At the first stage, all papers were evaluated and reviewed by the conference or Program Committee co-chairs. At the second stage, papers were evaluated and reviewed by at least one reviewer and the Program Committee members of the conference. At the third stage, we conducted a technical review and checked all papers for plagiarism, the level of researchers' English language proficiency, and the overall structure. As a result, we received a pool of high-quality papers, which presented best practices and scientific results related to the conference topics.

The plenary meeting's agenda included the presentations of the conference keynote speakers.

Cristina Sousa, PhD in Economics, Director of REMIT, Assistant Professor at Universidade Portucalense, focused on essential problems and effects of digital transformation.

Mohammed Berawi, Doctor of Philosophy, Associate Professor, Director of the Center for Sustainable Infrastructure Development (CSID), Universitas Indonesia, discussed the development of mega-infrastructure projects, the increasing feasibility of a project, and the value adding process.

Irina A. Rudskaya, Doctor of Economics, Associate Professor of the Graduate School of Engineering and Economics at the Institute of Industrial Management, Economics and Trade, SPbPU, presented some results of the empirical research on the interrelation between regional university complexes and the innovative development of the regions in Russia.

We would like to thank our keynote speakers, panelists, and authors, who contributed to the conference and made it possible by submitting and reviewing, according to the reviewers' comments. We are grateful to the members of the conference Program Committee for providing valuable and profound reviews. In addition, we wish to thank the Academic Excellence Project 5–100 proposed by Peter the Great St. Petersburg Polytechnic University for the financial support of this conference.

We hope that the conference will become an annual event to share recent developments in the sphere of the digital economy.

July 2020

Dmitrii Rodionov
Tatiana Kudryavtseva
Mohammed Ali Berawi
Angi Skhvediani

Organization

Conference Chairs

Vladimir Schepinin	Peter the Great St. Petersburg Polytechnic University, Russia
Dmitrii Rodionov	Peter the Great St. Petersburg Polytechnic University, Russia

Program Committee Chairs

Irina Rudskaya	Peter the Great St. Petersburg Polytechnic University, Russia
Tatiana Kudryavtseva	Peter the Great St. Petersburg Polytechnic University, Russia

Conference Program Committee

Alexey Bataev	Peter the Great St. Petersburg Polytechnic University, Russia
Anis Alamshoyev	Tajik State Finance and Economics University, Tajikistan
Angela Mottaeva	Moscow State University of Civil Engineering, Russia
Antonio Petruzzelli	Polytechnic University of Bari, Italy
Carlo Castellanelli	University of Aveiro, Portugal
Cristina Sousa	Universidade Portucalense, Portugal
Ekaterina Plotnikova	Peter the Great St. Petersburg Polytechnic University, Russia
Elena Sharafanova	St. Petersburg State University of Economics, Russia
Emma Ayensa	La Rioja University, Spain
Gregory Porumbescu	Rutgers University, USA
Isti Surjandari	Universitas Indonesia, Indonesia
Juan Hincapié	Universidad de Medellín, Colombia
Kulwant Pawar	University of Nottingham, UK
Marco Avarucci	University of Glasgow, UK
Marina Järvis	Tallinn University of Technology, Estonia
Maria Mißler-Behr	Brandenburg University of Technology, Germany
Mohammed Berawi	Universitas Indonesia, Indonesia
Natalya Kulagina	Bryansk State Engineering and Technology University, Russia
Oleg Kazakov	Bryansk State Engineering and Technology University, Russia

Olga Kalinina	Peter the Great St. Petersburg Polytechnic University, Russia
Pablo Quezada-Sarmiento	Universidad Politecnica de Madrid, Spain
Peeter Müürsepp	Tallinn University of Technology, Estonia
Ramayah Thurasamy	Universiti Malaysia Sarawak, Malaysia
Sergey Demin	Moscow Aviation Institute, National Research University, Russia
Tamara Shabunina	Institute for Problems of Regional Economics of the RAS, Russia
Yi Zhang	University of Technology Sydney, Australia

Technical Support Chair

| Angi Skhvediani | Peter the Great St. Petersburg Polytechnic University, Russia |

Technical Support Team

Anastasia Kulachinskaya	Peter the Great St. Petersburg Polytechnic University, Russia
Darya Kryzhko	Peter the Great St. Petersburg Polytechnic University, Russia
Natalia Abramchikova	Peter the Great St. Petersburg Polytechnic University, Russia

Contents

Economic Efficiency and Social Consequences of Digital Innovations Implementation

Developing a Mechanism for Assessing Cyber Risks in Digital Technology Projects Implemented in an Industrial Enterprise

Sergei Grishunin[1] , Svetlana Suloeva[2]([✉]) , and Ekaterina Burova[2]

[1] National Research University Higher School of Economics, Moscow, Russia
sgrishunin@hse.ru
[2] Peter the Great St. Petersburg Polytechnic University, St. Petersburg, Russia
{suloeva_sb,burova_ev}@spbstu.ru

Abstract. This study discusses the development of a mechanism for assessing cyber risks in investment projects aimed at digitalizing industrial enterprises. The relevance of the study is determined by the increasing susceptibility of companies to cyber risks due to the introduction of innovations, as well as by the growing complexity and frequency of cyber threats. The study focuses on eliminating the methodological and functional problems of cyber risk assessment described in literature. The results include the development of a concept for the mechanism and its architecture, the structural and logical scheme of the mechanism, and the specifications of the blocks it comprises. The theoretical and methodological basis of the research is formed on the works of foreign and Russian researchers in the field of corporate finance, risk management and cyber security. When building the mechanism, risk control approaches were used to ensure an inextricable connection between the risk factors and the goals of a project. The following tools were used: (1) a bow-tie chart for risk identification; (2) statistical data analysis methods; (3) risk-oriented budgeting and simulation modelling using the Monte-Carlo method; and (4) the "Micromort" method for evaluating the probability distribution parameters. In comparison to analogues, the mechanism represents an integrated approach to risk management and ensures integration and coordination of risk management actions between project management and other information security services. It allows the confidence intervals of return on invested capital values to be calculated for a project with due regard of cyber risks at the planning stage, as well as to identify and prioritize the degree of influence the main sources of threats have, which, as a result, provides a comprehensive and objective assessment of cyber risks. The calculation data can be used by project managers to enhance risk management actions. The functionality of the mechanism includes the analysis of how individual cyber risks affect the goals of a project, consideration of correlations between risks, calculation of the expected, unexpected and critical level of losses and forecasting in circumstances where information is limited. These advantages make the risk assessment process dynamic, iterative, and reactive to the changes in the environment and to the appearance of new threats.

Keywords: Cyber risks · Integrated risk management · Risk controlling · Economic profit · Industrial cybersecurity · Simulation modelling · Quantitative risk management

© Springer Nature Switzerland AG 2020
D. Rodionov et al. (Eds.): SPBPU IDE 2019, CCIS 1273, pp. 3–18, 2020.
https://doi.org/10.1007/978-3-030-60080-8_1

1 Introduction

Digitalization in production industry contributes to growing profitability and value of enterprises due to optimized value chains, reduced operational and investment costs, less time spent on launching new products, customized products and other advantages. However, these innovations increase the susceptibility of companies to cyber risks, whose number and frequency are forever growing [1–3].

In order to ensure effective counteracting against these threats, the mechanism used for assessing information security risks in digital innovation projects has to be further improved. It must represent an objective quantitative evaluation of the impact that cyber risks have on project goals, ensure integration and coordination of all actions aimed at assessing cyber risks and help to develop effective strategies for managing these risks. However, literature review proves that most of the existing mechanisms for assessing information security risks, for instance those based on OCTAVE, TARA or FAIR methodology, solve these problems only to a point.

This research is aimed at developing a mechanism for assessing cyber risks in project activity related to the introduction of digital technology in industrial enterprises. It is built on risk controlling principles and eliminates methodological and functional drawbacks in cyber risk assessment discussed in literature. The mechanism ensures an integrated approach to risk assessment as well as the integration and coordination of risk assessment with all risk management processes. The mechanism simulates the confidence interval of the predicted value for the return on invested capital (ROIC) indicator of a project and calculates the probabilities of going outside the limits of the permissible values of cyber risks for a company. For reference, the analogues represent just a pin-point (and frequently expert assessment) of how cyber risks affect the project indicators. The mechanism also allows you to make projections when statistics on risks are limited.

The study has the following structure. The second section discusses the need for managing cyber risks related to project activity in an industrial enterprise. The third part reviews literature relevant to the research. The fourth section considers the advantages of risk controlling in managing cyber risks. The fifth section presents the structural and logical scheme of the mechanism and the description of its main blocks and tools. The sixth section discusses the main benefits of the mechanism. The seventh section contains the conclusion and discussion of further research.

2 Relevance of Cyber Risk Management in Digital Technology Projects in Production Industry

Many researchers highlight that production activities in the 21st century are affected by a new spiral of scientific and technical progress [4–6]. This spiral is caused by the "fourth industrial revolution", which comprises of pass-through digitalization and automation of the entire value chain in a company to increase its efficiency. The key driver of Industry 4.0 is digital technology, including electronic devices, systems, tools and resources designed for data creation, storage and transfer (see Fig. 1). These are used by production objects to interact with each other via the Internet and transfer data about their state, status and other attributes. Digitalization in production industry is forming a cyber physical environment aimed at optimizing value chains, cutting production and investment costs, improving product quality, reducing time spent on launching new products and developing customized products. It changes enterprise management paradigms, since production processes can now be managed remotely or even virtually. This is going to increase the speed and quality of managerial decisions and allow staff optimization [7, 8].

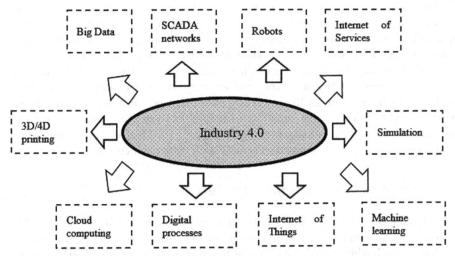

Fig. 1. Examples of digital technology in production industry. Source: developed by the authors

According to the consultants from PWC, in the nearest 4 years the market of Industry 4.0 will be growing with the compound annual growth rate (CAGR) being 16%–18% and can reach 150 billion USD by 2024. Introducing promising technologies such as 5G can speed up this growth. Increased productivity due to digitalization will ensure up to 14% increment in the world GDP by 2030, which is equivalent to 15 trillion USD[1].

However, in addition to the opportunities, digitalization poses new threats. The challenges are serious and can reduce investing in digital technology. The range of risks is wide and includes the absence of single standards for working with data, fears of growing unemployment rate, lack of infrastructure and equipment, operational problems, lack of trained personnel and immaturity of digital regulation. However, the interviews of the executives of industrial enterprises conducted by the company KMPG show that 68% of them believe that information security risks (cyber risks) are the most dangerous[2]. The specific features of digitalization in production industry are physical systems integrated with the Internet and distributed production eco-systems, making them vulnerable to cyber-attacks. They include (1) distributed attacks resulting in denial of service (DDOS); (2) data theft; (3) reconnaissance attacks; (4) man in the middle attacks; (5)

---

[1] Price Waterhouse Coopers. Industry 4.0: Global Digital Operations Study 2018 – Digital Champions. https://www.pwc.com/gx/en/industries/industry-4-0.html.

[2] KPMG. Global Manufacturing Outlook: Transforming for a digitally connected future 2018. https://assets.kpmg/content/dam/kpmg/xx/pdf/2018/06/global-manufacturing-outlook.pdf.

manipulation of production processes; (6) viruses and Trojan horses, etc. [1, 2]. Cyber threats in production industry (1) are systemic: one infected device opens the entire enterprise and its eco-system for an attack; and (2) can entail losses of third parties in case the enterprise is used as a middle man in the attack [1, 8, 10–12]. If the impact of cyber threats is not assessed objectively in the course of developing digital technology, it results in annual losses of the enterprise from risk realization within a range of 4 to 73 million dollars, depending on the type of attack[3].

The growing susceptibility to cyber threats, the emergence of the new vectors of attack and the complication of the existing ones make executives reconsider their approaches and mechanisms for assessing cyber risks in project activity related to digital technology development and introduction. New requirements are: (1) maximizing the ROIC from carrying out a project with due regard to cyber threats; (2) coordinating the roles and responsibility in the course of assessment; (3) predicting the distribution of deviations from the target ROIC as early as at the stage when design solutions are adopted; and (4) ensuring measurability of the influence of cyber threats on the target value of the ROIC at all stages of a project [1, 3, 10, 13–15]. But do the existing mechanisms for cyber risk assessment comply with these requirements?

3   Cyber Risk Management: Literature Review

Literature [1–3, 9, 11, 12, 16, 17] presents a big variety of risk assessment mechanisms, which we conditionally divided into (1) qualitative assessment mechanisms; (2) models for evaluating the maturity level of risk management systems (RMS); (3) risk management standards; and (4) quantitative assessment models.

The main advantage of qualitative models for analyzing operational security risks, such as OCTAVE (operationally critical threat-asset-asset-vulnerability evaluation), TARA (threat assessment and remediation analysis) [18, 19] or CyFMEA (cyber failure mode and effect analysis) [11, 12], is a holistic integrated approach to assessing. These models are also low-cost and can be used by project managers who have no serious specialized training. Qualitative assessment also implies that the mechanism can be used to assess new or emerging risks for which no statistics are available. These benefits allow us to use the mechanisms in small and medium enterprises with a small number of connections between digital devices. However, the reverse side of these mechanisms is their serious constraints. They imply only qualitative interpretation of risk probability and potential damage from risks. The result of applying the mechanisms is a risk map. Thomas et al. [20] highlight the following non-removable constraints of risk maps: (1) scalar (point) risk assessment; (2) complications in evaluating the correlations between risks; (3) instability due to categorization; (4) mean correction distortion; (5) instability of ranking categories; (6) spontaneous ranking by categories; (7) estimate compression by range. The mechanisms are also unsuitable for (1) evaluating the damage in monetary terms; (2) assessing the impact of the implemented risks on the key performance indicators (KPI) of projects; (3) "tracking" the entire risk chain from the attack vectors to

---

[3] Deloitte. Predicting the future of cyber security in Finnish manufacturing. https://www2. deloitte.com/content/dam/Deloitte/fi/Documents/risk/Cyber%20Secure%20Manufacturing% 20in%202021.pdf.

the KPI. The considered mechanisms can be enhanced due to (1) integrating monetary damage assessments in the mechanism; or (2) applying fuzzy logic to improve the interpretation of expert evaluations [21]. In our opinion these improvements only partially overcome the afore-mentioned disadvantages.

The advantage of the models and mechanisms for evaluating the maturity level of risk management systems, such as CMMI, Exostart or CRAMM [11] is a comprehensive assessment of the maturity of RMS. They can be used to compare the current degree of development of all elements of a project RMS and their interconnections with the desirable status of the RMS, determine the gaps between them and build up a road map to advance the system. However, all these mechanisms are designed to find weaknesses in the RMS rather than evaluate the effect produced by the risks that have been incurred in the weak points on the KPI of a project. So these mechanisms are applied to analyze the reliability of the information security system. The mechanisms can be reinforced if they are combined with mechanism that directly measure risks. An example of such combination is the CRAM mechanism (CCTA risk analysis and management method). It can be used to assess the maturity degree of equipment information security, to analyze risks based on expert evaluations given to resources, threats and vulnerabilities of resources and to prepare a control system of these risks. However, the methodology of risk assessment in GRAMM is similar to the approaches used in qualitative risk analysis models, so it has most of the disadvantages described above.

Mechanisms, based on risk management standards such as ISO 27001 or NIST [22, 23], represent a holistic approach to risk management, since they combine all the necessary components: goal-setting, risk analysis, developing strategies to react to risks, control over incurred risks and taking counter-management decisions. The standards, underlying these mechanisms, are recognized all over the world. They are forever developing and being updated [11]. Their shortcoming is a descriptive character, i.e. they explain what has to be done but do not provide any concrete risk assessment and management tools.

The mechanisms for quantitative assessment of cyber risks are based on stochastic models (SMs), such as cyber value at risk (CyVAR), designed by FAIR [11] or RISKEE [21]. These models use the theory of probabilities to calculate the confidence interval of the damage resulting from information security risks for a set period of time [11]. The strong points of SMs are (1) monetary evaluation of damage; (2) using simulation modelling with lots of scenarios; (3) presenting the expected, unexpected and critical level of losses. For instance, the RISKEE mechanism, developed by Krisper, et. al. [21], determines the resulting damage in the following way: (1) building an attack tree; (2) using expert evaluation of attributes of a risk event; and (3) calculating the damage directly using a Monte-Carlo method. The advantage of this approach is combining the failure tree analysis model (FTA) and FAIR approach, which allows us to "track" the connections between the damage and the factors of attack vectors. Nevertheless, this mechanism has drawbacks, too: (1) it cannot be used to track the effect of damage from cyber risks on project efficiency; (2) it represents a RMS tool, rather than a comprehensive RMS, which can be used to determine strategies for reacting to risk and to control risk implementation.

Thus, according to the analysis we can conclude that the mechanisms described in literature have constraints. It prevents them from getting adapted to assess cyber threats in projects that are implemented in a complex and rapidly changing environment. One of the solutions to the problem is to use risk controlling, an integrated risk management system of a new generation in an industrial enterprise.

4   Risk Controlling as an Up-to-Date System of Integrated Risk Management

Risk Controlling (RC) is a goal-oriented system of integrated risk management for organizing risk management in the processes of planning, analysis and assessment, control and accounting, industry engineering and regulation, including project activities [24–26]. RC is aimed at creating and supporting the architecture of a risk management system: concept, organization, methodologies, methods, processes and tools of risk management. Applying this architecture to specific risks such as, for example, information security risks, project managers, in a course of self-controlling, determine the effect of these risks on the goals of the project and carry out risk-oriented control of the project. The functions of risk controlling are specified in [24–26]. The advantages of RC are: (1) solving problems related to coordinating and integrating risk management actions both inside the system and in relation to other control loops; (2) ensuring an inextricable connection between risks, their factors and causes, on the one hand, and strategic and operational goals of the enterprise or the project, on the other hand; (3) focusing on early risk identification and control; (4) using "high-precision" tools aimed at making assessment more accurate [26].

As for digitalization projects, information security risk controlling is aimed at reducing the risks that the project will fail to reach its objectives (for example, target ROIC). The specific feature of digitalization projects in production industry is their great complexity and lots of interconnected equipment. The need to ensure a large quantity of inputs and outputs for data acquisition (including into the external environment of the enterprise), transferring some functions into digital eco-systems (which are poorly controlled by the enterprise), balancing between security and compatibility make the enterprise an easy target for cyber criminals. The harder the project, the more likely the negative deviation of the actually achieved value of ROIC in comparison with the target one [24, 25].

In order to evaluate the effect of information security risks on project efficiency, we developed the indicator cyber ROIC (CyROIC). It measures the return on capital invested into the project at time t

$$CyROIC_t = \frac{(NOPAT_t - L_t \times MR_t - CIT_t)}{IC_t} \tag{1}$$

Where: $NOPAT_t$ is the net operating profit from project implementation, L_t is the estimated damage from information security risk incurrence, MR_t is the share of unavoidable damage due to risk management actions, IC_t – is the capital invested in the project at time t, CIT_t is the operating costs on maintaining the cyber security system.

In its turn, the invested capital will be determined by the total capital invested into the project at time t, namely:

$$IC_t = E_t + D_t \tag{2}$$

Where: E_t, D_t are the share of equity and debt capital invested into the project at time t, considering investments into the cyber security system.

At time t the project will be cost-efficient and increase the value of the company (i.e. it will have a positive economic profit) if the profitability of the project exceeds the costs of invested capital [27]:

$$EVA_t = (CyROIC_t - WACC_t) \times IC_t \tag{3}$$

Where: $WACC_t$ is the weighted average capital cost over period t.

In its turn, the cost-efficiency of the project over the entire period of its useful life (T) will be determined from the ratio:

$$MVA = \sum_{t=1}^{T} \frac{EVA_t}{(1 + WACC_t)^t} \tag{4}$$

Where MVA is the efficiency of the project considering the effect of information security risks.

The advantages of the CyROIC indicator are: (1) possibility to calculate the return on invested capital considering the possibility of cyber risk incurrence and the need for additional capital investment and costs of cyber security; (2) strong correlation with changes in project efficiency; (3) measurability at all levels of the project; and (4) applicability for framing awards for project managers. However, for an objective reflection of the effect that cyber threats have on ROIC, a mechanism is needed to identify risk factors, carry out scenario analysis of the probabilities and effects of risk incurrence and determine the impact of these consequences.

5   Developing a Mechanism for Assessing Cyber Risks in the Project Activities of an Industrial Enterprise

5.1   The Structural and Logical Scheme of the Mechanism. Creating Architecture for Cyber Risk Management

The structural and logical scheme of the developed mechanism is presented in Fig. 2.

For the mechanism to work effectively, the company needs the right architecture for cyber risk management. Its purpose is to reduce the effect of risks due to organizational and operating sponsorship. This architecture implies that the project participants are divided into groups in charge of cyber risk management activities. Each groups forms its "line of defense" against risks, and each participant of the group has specific goals and objectives.

In the suggested mechanism, the architecture of cyber risk management consists of four lines of defense. The first line consists of project managers. They are responsible for (1) risk identification and assessment, development and implementation of

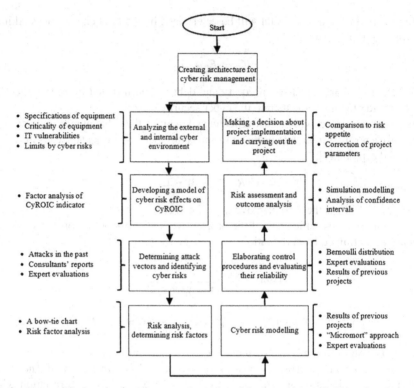

Fig. 2. Chart of the mechanism for assessing cyber risks in project activities of an industrial enterprise. Source: developed by the authors

counter-management actions; (2) development and support of control procedures; (3) communication on risks and current risk monitoring. The second line of defense includes controllers who carry out the main actions for methodological and coordination support of the first line of defense in terms of cyber risk management, tools provision and consulting. The third line of defense includes the functions of corporate support (compliance, legal department, human resources, security department, accounting department). Its objective is internal control over project efficiency within the experts' scope of competence, as well as monitoring the compliance with legislation, quality control and financial control. The goal of the third line of defense is to make sure that all elements of risk management in the project work effectively and prevent threats. Finally, the fourth line of defense is the internal audit department. It has to carry out an independent check-up of the efficiency of all departments and the entire mechanism, including the operating efficiency of control procedures. Audit is usually conducted as retrospective analysis after the project is completed.

5.2   Analyzing the External and Internal Cyber Environment of a Project

The first stage of the mechanism is to analyze the internal and external cyber environment of the project. The main ideas of this analysis are (1) evaluating the criticality of the developed digital equipment and its parts for the company; (2) determining the vulnerability of this equipment to cyber-attacks. In order to solve the first task, a ranking model can be applied [25]. It is used for comprehensive analysis of the equipment by critical factors, with each of them having an expert weight assigned depending on the importance of the factor. Technical and operating parameters of assets are the input data for the model.

In order to solve the second task, the maturity level of the company's information security risk management system as a whole is evaluated during the first step [22, 23, 31]. A maturity model is used for this purpose. It identifies weaknesses in cyber security risk management and assesses how critical they are. According to the results of this analysis, a strategy must be developed to make cyber risk management more efficient.

The second step is to use scanning software, simulating various scenarios of cyber-attacks on digital equipment. The sources of information for such scenarios are (1) publications of respected organizations in the field of information security, including Verizon, Symantec, FireEye [24]; (2) analysis of the internal or external databases of previous cyber incidents; (3) scientific research [34]; and (4) expert evaluations (less preferable). According to the results of simulation, vulnerabilities in the weak points of the equipment are identified, and their essentiality and potential losses for the company are assessed.

The main outcome of the analyzed external and internal environment is revealing all factors determining CyROIC and interconnections between them. This information can be used in factor analysis to build a mathematical model of CyROIC. Moreover, at this stage the minimal admissible value of project CyROIC is defined (project risk appetite - $CyROIC_R$), which is acceptable for the company. Its is characterized by the probability of achievement (δ), which the company sets on its own account (for example, 90%) [29].

5.3 Cyber Risk Identification and Primary Analysis

At the next stage, based on the data acquired when the internal and external cyber environment was analyzed, the potential attack vectors are determined for the revealed vulnerabilities and final cyber risks are finally identified. The attack vectors are analyzed using attack trees [32]. The outcome of the analysis is building a cyber risk register. For each risk it must present (1) a detailed risk description; (2) the type and purpose of the attack happening in a course of risk incurrence; (3) the characteristics of the attack initiator; (4) the point of penetration and a set of rights required for this; and (5) the described mechanism of the attack.

5.4 Risk Modelling and Analysis

According to the results of the analyzed attack tree, each cyber risk from the register is broken down to risk factors [32]. At the same time, the impact of the risk on the factors comprising CyROIC is determined. The tool for visualizing this process is a bow-tie chart (Fig. 3) [29].

The right part of the chart represents the CyROIC model built during analysis of the internal and external cyber environment. The left part of the chart is a graph, whose nodes are risk factors (C_i). All nodes are connected with each other with cause-and-effect

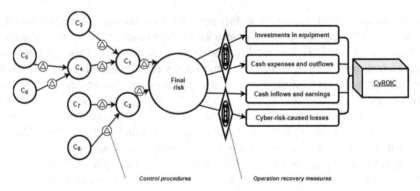

Fig. 3. A bow-tie chart for risk factor analysis. Source: [29]

relations. The final risk is the central link of the chart. The probability of the final risk is preconditioned by the probabilities of the risk factors.

The probability of each risk depends on the probabilities of the risk factors which it consists of. Various models can be used to model the probability of the final risk, with most widely-spread being probability models of epidemic outbreaks [33]; or Bayesian networks [30]. The ways of assessing the probability distribution of the risk factors, suggested in the mechanism, are given in Fig. 4.

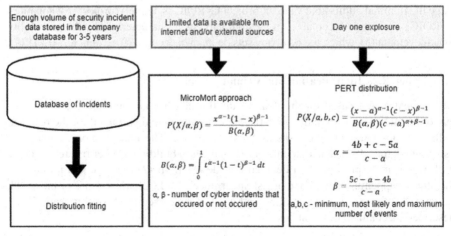

Fig. 4. Approach to evaluating the probability distribution of cyber risk factors. Sources: [11, 17, 35]

The final stage of risk analysis is to determine the places of location and to design control procedures. They are aimed at either preventing a risk factor from incurring (a "barrier" control procedure), or identifying the incurrence of a risk factor early ("an identifying control procedure"). A bow-tie chart is also used in order to discover the connection between control procedures and risk factors and to decide on the places of control procedures (Fig. 3).

When choosing the best design for each control procedure, the probability of its failure (i.e. the inability to prevent in due time a risk factor from incurring) should be evaluated. The mechanism suggests using either a Bernoulli distribution or a PERT distribution as a probability distribution function to assess the inefficiency of control procedures. The parameters of these distributions are determined either on the basis of statistics on the failures detected in control work during previous projects, or in an expert way in case there are no such statistics [29].

5.5 Risk Assessment and Outcome Analysis

Risks are assessed by simulation modelling using Monte-Carlo methods [17, 28, 36]. The goal is to calculate the CyROIC confidence interval considering the susceptibility of the project to cyber threats. The methodology of confidence interval calculation is similar to the "value at risk" methodology (VAR), which is applied in financial management [28, 29, 36]. The proposed mechanism carries out simulation modelling using the MS Excel spreadsheet package with the installed ModelRisk application[4].

During the first step, the correlation between the identified cyber risks is evaluated. To do so, you should either use historically observed correlations between similar risks in the previous projects, or use expert opinions (in case there are no statistics for the previous years or if new risks have been identified). During the second step, all bow-tie charts obtained at the previous stage are consolidated with the help of the MS Excel facilities considering the cyber risks correlated with each other. During the third stage, simulation modelling is carried out, descriptive CyROIC statistics are calculated, and visual graphs are built to analyze the results and take decisions about project implementation or rejection.

The key graph in the outcome analysis is the bar chart showing the distribution of the projected ROIC values with due regard of cyber threats (Fig. 5). It allows us to evaluate (1) the expected deviations of the CyROIC indicator from the initial plan; (2) the most probable CyROIC value as a result of project implementation; (3) the probability of CyROIC reducing below the value of $CyROIC_R$ risk appetite. The bar chart can also be used to determine the probability of achieving the desirable value of the CyROIC indicator.

In addition, the project team can identify which cyber risks and their factors can make the biggest contribution into the expected CyROIC deviation from the plan. A tornado diagram is used to do so [28, 29].

If the analyzed results of modelling demonstrate that the lower limit of the CyROIC δ-confidence interval is below the value of the $CyROIC_R$ risk appetite, then the project is inefficient in terms of susceptibility to cyber threats and should either be terminated or improved. This improvement implies that vulnerabilities are eliminated, the design of control procedures is added or changed, and the operating efficiency of control procedures is increased. After that simulation modelling is repeated to check up whether the expected CyROIC value is within the limits of the risk appetite. Moreover, the outcome analysis helps to discover (1) the amounts of the reserves in case unfavorable scenarios unfold; (2) on which key risk zones the focus should be.

---

[4] https://www.vosesoftware.com/products/modelrisk/.

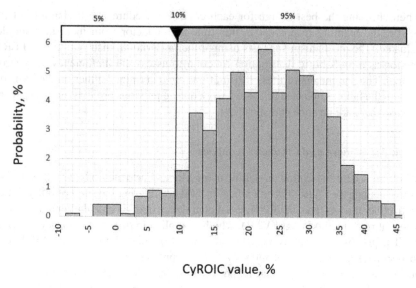

Fig. 5. Bar chart of projected CyROIC distribution, %.

In conclusion, it should be noted that the process of cyber risk assessment in digitalization projects must be carried out either on a regular basis or in case the main stages of the project are completed. After the project is finished, all steps aimed at assessing cyber risks and the specifications of the counter-management actions must be documented and submitted to the internal audit department so that the efficiency of the actions taken can be evaluated. The objective of internal audit is to develop guidelines to improve the process of risk assessment for future projects.

6 Advantages of the Developed Mechanism Over the Existing Analogues

The developed mechanism has considerable advantages over the analogues discussed in Sect. 3, both the ones suggesting qualitative or determinate quantitative risk assessment (CRAMM, OCTAVE, TARA, COBIT for Risk, etc.) and the ones suggesting stochastic quantitative risk assessment (for instance, FAIR). The characteristics of the developed mechanism are compared to those of their analogues in Table 1.

These advantages confirm the high practical applicability of the developed mechanism. The projections carried out using the model are statistically valid and can increase the efficiency of business due to detailed assessment of cyber threats and development of effective actions to manage these threats. The trial of the mechanism in consulting projects demonstrated the possibility of reducing the deviations from the target ROIC values in projects by 20%–30%.

Table 1. Advantages of the developed mechanism in comparison with analogues

The mechanism presented	Analogues	Type of analogues
Suggests using a holistic integrated approach to risk assessment, embracing all aspects of assessment and their connection with other risk management elements, including decision-making on the development of a strategy to manage cyber risks and project value	Fragmented approaches that do not represent a comprehensive subsystem of the general integrated risk management system. They often represent a set of isolated tools and are not integrated in decision-making activity related to risk management and project value management	All
Ensures coordinated risk assessment activity, contributes to the development of risk culture	Insufficient determination of risk management roles and responsibilities, weak communication and coordination between roles, lack of focus on risk culture	All
Assesses probabilities of exceeding the level of risk tolerance and risk appetite	Do not assess the chances of going outside the limits of risk appetite	All
Multi-factor stochastic risk assessment, building the confidence interval of the ROIC indicator and assessing the probability of achieving the target indicators	Qualitative (expert) evaluation and simultaneous projecting with further analysis of sensitivity. The probability of achieving the target indicators is not assessed	Qualitative
Ensures clear interconnection between uncertainty factors, risks, financial indicators and the ROIC indicator	Do not track or track only partially the connection between risk factors, risks, financial indicators and project target indicators	Qualitative
Application of the Monte-Carlo method for simulating a large number of scenarios	Limited number of scenarios	Qualitative
Can be used to analyze the contribution of individual risks and their factors in the deviation of the ROIC indicator	Cannot be used to "track" the contribution of each risk and its component risk factors in the deviation of indicators from the target	Qualitative
Considers correlations in risk aggregation, assesses the effect of aggregate risks on the ROIC indicators.	Limited, frequently qualitative consideration of interactions between risks	Qualitative

(continued)

Table 1. (*continued*)

The mechanism presented	Analogues	Type of analogues
Can be used to consider risk change in dynamics	As a rule, static risk assessment	Qualitative
Can be used to run stress-test with various combinations of risks and component factors	Analysis of sensitivity to individual risks or component factors	Qualitative
Sets a clear forecasting period	Difficulties in clear determination of the forecasting period	Qualitative
Can be used to model the probability of failures in control procedures	Cannot be used to model the probability of failures in control procedures	Quantitative
A wide range of probability distributions for the purposes of modelling	Smaller range of probability distributions (as a rule, PERT)	Quantitative
Makes it possible to use the Micro Mort approach and calculate probabilities on a small amount of statistics	Need considerable amounts of statistics to evaluate the distribution parameters	Quantitative

7 Conclusion and Further Research

Together with increasing efficiency, digitalization in production industry entails considerable information security risks. In order to improve the efficiency of their assessment, we developed a mechanism for assessing cyber risks in digital technology projects in an industrial enterprise. The advantages of the mechanism is a holistic integrated approach to risk assessment, as well as coordination of all steps of risk assessment with other elements of information security risk management. It includes effective tools and methods which can be used to (1) quantitatively assess cyber risks and determine their total level; (2) establish clear interrelation between uncertainty factors, risks, financial indicators and the indicator of return on capital invested into the project (ROIC); and (3) forecast ROIC deviations from the strategic plan at all stages of the project.

The main areas of further research are, firstly, further development of the mechanism for forming a full-fledged integrated risk controlling subsystem to manage information security risks. Secondly, the mechanism should be adapted to projects aimed at developing certain types of innovations (for example, the Industrial Internet of Things, automated control and data acquisition systems, etc.). Thirdly, the mechanism should be adjusted to agile ways of project management. Finally, the research should be aimed at further increasing the efficiency of the tools and methods used in the mechanism. They include (1) selecting the optimal probability distributions for various types of information security risks; (2) developing cause-and-effect networks to analyze the causes and sources of risks; (3) enhancing the models for predicting actions (4) developing a system of key indicators anticipating cyber threats.

Acknowledgements. This research work was supported by the Academic Excellence Project 5–100 proposed by Peter the Great St. Petersburg Polytechnic University.

References

1. Antonucci, D.: The Cyber Risk Handbook: Creating and Measuring Effective Cyber-Security capabilities. Wiley, Hoboken (2017)
2. Refsdal, A., Solhaug, B., Stolen, K.: Cyber-Risk Management. Springer, Cham (2015). https://doi.org/10.1007/978-3-319-23570-7
3. Von Solms, R., Van Niekerk, J.: From information security to cyber security. Comput. Secur. **38**, 97–102 (2013)
4. Asaturova, J.: Peculiarities of development of industry 4.0 concept in Russia. In: IOP Conference Series: Materials Science and Engineering, vol. 497, no. 1 (2019)
5. Gromova, E.: Digital economy development with an emphasis on automotive industry in Russia. Espacios **40**(6) (2019)
6. Liao, Y., Loures, E., Deschamps, F., Ramos, L.F.: Past, present and future of industry 4.0 – a systematic literature review and research agenda proposal. Int. J. Prod. Res. **55**(12), 3609–3639 (2017)
7. Bataev, A.: Analysis and development the digital economy in the world. In: Proceedings of the 31st International Business Information Management Association Conference, pp. 61–71 (2018)
8. Rodionov, D., Rudskaia, I.: Problems of infrastructural development of "industry 4.0" in Russia on Sibur experience. In: Proceedings of the 32nd International Business Information Management Association Conference, pp. 3534–3544 (2018)
9. Cherdantseva, Y., et al.: Review of cyber security risk assessment methods for SCADA systems. Comput. Secur. **56**, 1–27 (2016)
10. Lam, J.: Enterprise Risk Management: From Incentives to Controls, 2nd edn. Wiley, Hoboken (2014)
11. Radanliev, P., et al.: Future developments in cyber risk assessment for the Internet of Things. Comput. Ind. **102**, 14–22 (2018)
12. Ralston, P.A.S., Graham, J.H., Hieb, J.L.: Cyber security risk assessment for SCADA and DCS networks. ISA Trans. **46**, 583–594 (2007)
13. Dvas, G., Dubolazova, Y.: Risk assessment and risk management of innovative activity of the enterprise. In: Proceedings of the 31st International Business Information Management Association Conference, pp. 5650–5653 (2018)
14. Rodionov, D., Afanasyeva, N., Nikolova, L.: Impact of globalization on innovation project risks estimation. Eur. Res. Stud. J. **20**(2), 396–410 (2017)
15. Rodionov, D., Konnikova, O., Konnikov, E.: Approaches to ensuring the sustainability of industrial enterprises of different technological levels. J. Soc. Sci. Res. **3**, 277–282 (2018)
16. Dazhong, W., et al.: Cybersecurity for digital manufacturing. J. Manuf. Syst. (2018). https://doi.org/10.1016/j.jmsy.2018.03.006
17. Hubbard, D., Seiersen, R.: How to Measure Anything in Cybersecurity Risk. Wiley, Hoboken (2016)
18. Caralli, R., Stevens, J., Young, L., Wilson, W.: Introducing OCTAVE: improving the information security risk assessment process. Hansom AFB, MA (2007)
19. Wynn, J., et al.: Threat assessment and remediation analysis methodology. Bedford (2011)
20. Thomas, P., Bratvold, R., Bickel, J.E.: The risk of using risk matrices. Soc. Pet. Eng. Econ. Manag. **6**(2), 56–66 (2014)

21. Krisper, M., Dobaj, J., Macher, G., Schmittner, C.: RISKEE: a risk-tree based method for assessing risk in cyber security. In: Walker, A., O'Connor, R.V., Messnarz, R. (eds.) EuroSPI 2019. CCIS, vol. 1060, pp. 45–56. Springer, Cham (2019). https://doi.org/10.1007/978-3-030-28005-5_4

22. ISO/IEC 27005:2013 Information Technology - Security Techniques - Information Security Risk Management. International Organization for Standardization and International Electrotechnical Commission, Homepage. https://www.iso.org/standard/75281.html. Accessed 11 June 2019

23. Kline, J.J., Hutchins, G.: Enterprise risk management: a global focus on standardization. Glob. Bus. Organ. Excel. **36**(6), 44–53 (2017)

24. Grishunin, S., Suloeva, S.: Project controlling in telecommunication industry. In: Balandin, S., Andreev, S., Koucheryavy, Y. (eds.) ruSMART 2015. LNCS, vol. 9247, pp. 573–584. Springer, Cham (2015). https://doi.org/10.1007/978-3-319-23126-6_51

25. Andersen, D., Keleher, P., Smith, P.: Toward an assessment tool for the strategic management of asset criricality. Aust. J. Mech. Eng. **5**(2), 115–126 (2008)

26. Grishunin, S., Mukhanova, N., Suloeva, S.: Development of concept of risk controlling in industrial eneterprise. Organ. Prod. **26**(1), 45–56 (2018). (RUS)

27. Ivashkovskaya, I., Evdokimov, S.: Does corporate financial architecture of innovative companies differ? Evid. USA. J. Corp. Financ. Res. **12**(4), 7–28 (2018). https://doi.org/10.17323/j.jcfr.2073-0438.12.4.2018.7-28

28. Funston, F., Wagner, S.: Surviving and Thriving in Uncertainty. Creating the Risk Intelligent Enterprise. Wiley, Hoboken (2010)

29. Grishunin, S., Suloeva, S., Nekrasova, T.: Development of the mechanism of risk-adjusted scheduling and cost budgeting of R&D projects in telecommunications. In: Galinina, O., Andreev, S., Balandin, S., Koucheryavy, Y. (eds.) NEW2AN/ruSMART -2018. LNCS, vol. 11118, pp. 456–470. Springer, Cham (2018). https://doi.org/10.1007/978-3-030-01168-0_41

30. Kotenko, I., Chechulin, A.: A cyber attack modeling and impact assessment framework. In: Proceedings of 5th International Conference on Cyber Conflict (CYCON 2013), pp. 1–24 (2013)

31. Bahuguna, A., Bisht, R.K., Pande, J.: Assessing cybersecurity maturity of organizations: an empirical investigation in the Indian context. Inf. Secur. J. **28**(6), 164–177 (2019)

32. Ten, C.-W., Liu, C.-C., Govindarasu, M.: Vulnerability assessment of cybersecurity for SCADA systems using attack trees. In: Proceedings of IEEE Power Engineering Society General Meeting, PES, Tampa, FL, United States, 4275642 (2007)

33. Tiwari, V.K., Dwivedi, R.: Analysis of cyber attack vectors. In: Proceedings of IEEE International Conference on Computing, Communication and Automation, ICCCA 2016, Greater Noida, India, 7813791, pp. 600–604 (2016)

34. Irmak, E., Erkek, I.: An overview of cyber attack vectors on SCADA systems. In: Proceedings of 6th International Symposium on Digital Forensic and Security, ISDFS 2018, Antalya, Turkey, vol. 2018, pp. 1–5 (2018)

35. Radanliev, P., De Roure, D., Cannady, S., Montalvo, R.M., Nicolescu, R., Huth, M.: Economic impact of IoT cyber risk - analysing past and present to predict the future developments in IoT risk analysis and IoT cyber insurance. In: Proceedings of IET Conference Living in the Internet of Things: Cybersecurity of the IoT – 2018, London, United Kingdom, vol. 2018, Issue CP740 (2018)

36. Shourabi, N.B., Dean, R., Moazzami, F., Astatke, Y.: A model for cyber attack risks in telemetry networks. In: Proceedings of the International Telemetering Conference, vol. 82, pp. 691–700

Artificial Intelligence System for Processing Big Data to Determine the Value of Innovative Products in a Digital Economy

Nikolay Lomakin[1]($\boxtimes$) iD, Sergey Sazonov[1] iD, Alena Polianskaia[1] iD,
Gennady Lukyanov[2] iD, and Alina Gorbunova[2]

[1] Volgograd State Technical University, Volgograd 400005, Russian Federation
tel9033176642@yahoo.com
[2] Volga Polytechnic Institute (branch) of Volgograd State Technical University,
Volzhsky 404121, Russian Federation

Abstract. Theoretical foundations for artificial intelligence systems being applied in Big Data processing have been considered. Capabilities of the Hadoop framework and Deductor analytic platform have been analyzed and compared. A technology to mine data from news Web sites due to the developed Skraper program has been considered. There were discussed some issues, revealing capabilities of the Word2vec program that was used in scientific research and provided for the retrieved words being vectorized in a 300-dimension format.

An AI system has been proposed to predict the cost of innovative products of the Russian economy under conditions of digitalization. There has been put forward and proven a hypothesis that a neural network enables forecasting the cost of innovative products in the Russian Federation for the next quarter. The neural network is based on statistical indicators and economic parameters that reflect the dynamics of the financial and economic system in Russia, including the volume of innovative products quarterly for the period from 2015 to 2018.

There was also put forward and proven a hypothesis that the neural network allows predicting the cost of innovative products in the Russian Federation. The proposed solution is of great practical importance, since the developed AI-system is based on forecasting the volume of innovative products for the next quarter and provides identification of the economic growth potential. One of the parameters in the model takes into account the dynamics of the VIX option—the "fear index"—that reflects the investment activity in the global economy.

The multidimensional diagram based on the data quantization revealed the relationship between the Russian GDP trend and the cost of innovative products together with the stock quotation of the VIX option. The developed AI system allowed forecasting the cost of innovative products, using the "what-if" function for the next quarter in the Deductor platform.

Keywords: Innovative products · AI-system · Forecast · Hadoop · Deductor · Big data · Digitalization · Word2vec · Skraper

D. Rodionov et al. (Eds.): SPBPU IDE 2019, CCIS 1273, pp. 19–37, 2020.
https://doi.org/10.1007/978-3-030-60080-8_2

1   Introduction

1.1   Theoretical Basis of the Big Data Study

The relevance of the study is that the applicability of artificial intelligence is growing rapidly; however, certain problems that arise from the expansion require further research. The article touches upon the problem, the research studies of many scientists were devoted to, but its individual aspects have been insufficiently considered.

Theoretical foundations of the artificial intelligence system used in Big Data processing were studied. The capabilities of the Hadoop framework and Deductor analytic platform were analyzed and compared. The technology for mining data from news Web sites, using the developed Skraper program, was considered.

There were discussed some issues, characterizing capabilities of the Word2vec program that was used in scientific research and ensured the collected words, being vectorized in a 300-dimension format.

The authors proposed an AI system for predicting the cost of innovative products resulted from Big Data processing under economy digitalization.

There has been put forward and proven a hypothesis that a neural network enables forecasting the cost of innovative products in the Russian Federation. The proposed solution is of great practical importance, since the developed AI-system ensures identification of the economic growth potential based on the forecast of the volume of innovative products for the next quarter.

One of the parameters in the model considers the dynamics of the VIX option—the "fear index"—that reflects the investment activity in the global economy.

The multidimensional diagram based on the data quantization revealed the dependence of the Russian GDP trend on the cost of innovative products and stock quotation of a VIX option.

1.2   Big Data Analysis Tools

The data science and analytics to be created and promoted in terms of theoretical foundation, algorithms, models, evaluation, experiments, applications, and systems associated with specific issues were presented in the Data Analytics book. Being a brief study in the field of advanced information processing and knowledge, Springer Briefs book turned out to be very useful.

We know many programs, a huge variety of different platforms and tools to analyze Big Data. Some of them are frameworks (Hadoop, Spark, and Storm), databases (Hive, Impala, Presto, and Drill), analytical platforms (RapidMiner, IBM SPSS Modeler, KNIME, Qlik Analytics Platform, STATISTICA Data Miner, Informatica Intelligent Data Platform, World Programming System, Deductor, and SAS Enterprise Miner), and other tools (Zookeeper, Flume, IBM Watson Analytics, Dell EMC Analytic Insights Module, Windows Azure HDInsight, Microsoft Azure Machine Learning, Pentaho Data Integration, Tera data Aster Analytics, SAP Business Objects Predictive Analytics, Oracle Big Data Preparation etc.).

Hadoop is known to be an open source environment that includes several fragments (Fig. 1). So, each of the fragments is processed on any node (or computer) in a cluster of the computing system generated.

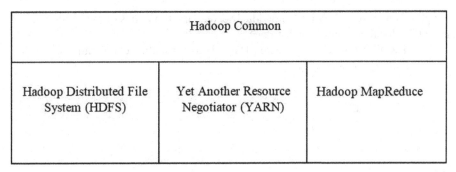

Hadoop Common		
Hadoop Distributed File System (HDFS)	Yet Another Resource Negotiator (YARN)	Hadoop MapReduce

Fig. 1. Hadoop logical representation

Deductor is an analytical platform that has a wide range of capabilities, including the development of neural networks such as perceptron, Kohonen map, data quantization, and others.

Parsing and scraping are known to be used for search and retrieving necessary information from the Internet.

The open-source Hadoop framework system used in the study made it possible to retrieve signals generated with a quarter time frame for the subsequent identification of innovative trends.

The scientific research had the task to develop a Scraper program that mines data of a certain time frame from a URL list of news websites. Based on the Hadoop parallel computing capabilities, words in the data fragments retrieved from web pages were calculated by the Scraper program. To obtain the desired result in the form of a "word, quantity" list, a program algorithm was developed. Its block diagram is presented below (Fig. 2).

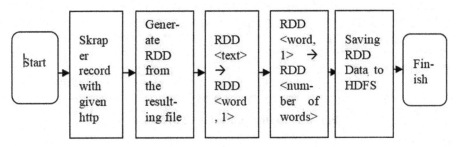

Fig. 2. Scraper cell chart

The role of the Hadoop software library consisted in it shaving wide capabilities, serving as an environment that allowed applying distributed processing of large data sets in computer clusters using simple models.

Spark is a unique open source framework for implementing distributed processing of unstructured data.

Spark is well scaled by both individual servers and thousands of machines; each of them offers local computing and storage.

To run RDD (Resilient Distributed Dataset) to parallelize computations, a Word-Count in Python was used (Fig. 3).

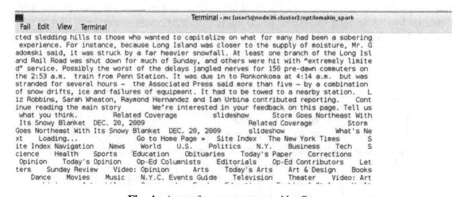

RDD API Examples

Word Count

In this example, we use a few transformations to build a dataset of (String, Int) pairs called counts and then save it to a file.

Python   Scala   Java

```
text_file = sc.textFile("hdfs://...")
counts = text_file.flatMap(lambda line: line.split(" ")) \
        .map(lambda word: (word, 1)) \
        .reduceByKey(lambda a, b: a + b)
counts.saveAsTextFile("hdfs://...")
```

Fig. 3. WordCount on Python

RDD—Resilient Distributed Dataset—is a core Spark concept and a key to understanding Spark.

The Scraper code is generated in Python. Using the Scraper software of any time frame we extracted texts; a fragment of one of them is presented below (Fig. 4).

```
Terminal - mc [user5@node39.cluster]:/opt/lomakin_spark
Fail  Edit  View  Terminal
cted sledding hills to those who wanted to capitalize on what for many had been a sobering
 experience. For instance, because Long Island was closer to the supply of moisture, Mr. G
adomski said, it was struck by a far heavier snowfall. At least one branch of the Long Isl
and Rail Road was shut down for much of Sunday, and others were hit with "extremely limite
d" service. Possibly the worst of the delays jangled nerves for 150 pre-dawn commuters on
the 2:53 a.m. train from Penn Station. It was due in to Ronkonkoma at 4:14 a.m. but was
stranded for several hours — the Associated Press said more than five — by a combination
of snow drifts, ice and failures of equipment. It had to be towed to a nearby station.   L
iz Robbins, Sarah Wheaton, Raymond Hernandez and Ian Urbina contributed reporting.   Cont
inue reading the main story     We're interested in your feedback on this page. Tell us
 what you think.     Related Coverage        slideshow     Storm Goes Northeast With
 Its Snowy Blanket  DEC. 20, 2009               Related Coverage        Storm
Goes Northeast With Its Snowy Blanket  DEC. 20, 2009        slideshow        What's Ne
xt    Loading...        Go to Home Page »  Site Index  The New York Times        S
ite Index Navigation    News    World    U.S.    Politics    N.Y.    Business    Tech    S
cience    Health    Sports    Education    Obituaries    Today's Paper    Corrections
 Opinion    Today's Opinion    Op-Ed Columnists    Editorials    Op-Ed Contributors    Let
ters    Sunday Review    Video: Opinion    Arts    Today's Arts    Art & Design    Books
    Dance    Movies    Music    N.Y.C. Events Guide    Television    Theater    Video: Art
```

Fig. 4. A text fragment extracted by Scraper

To parallelize computations by the RDD, we used Word Count in Python. The resulting unstructured text was then transformed, and the words were calculated using RDD <word, 1> --> RDD <word, number of words> (Fig. 5).

We used an open source program Word2vec and got initial data for a 300-dimension vector (Fig. 6).

Of great importance was the expedition of data processing.

In Case I, the Scraper program processed data when one worker and one thread were involved.

```
'', 1643)
('NYTimes.com', 3)
('no', 2)
('longer', 1)
('supports', 1)
('9', 1)
('Please', 4)
('browser.', 1)
('LEARN', 1)
('MORE', 1)
('B»', 2)
```

Fig. 5. Received file with counted words

```
0.01952848865177909; 0.00555642665624340; 0.00616401902728167; -0.01106280164728921; 0.02516122026790111; 0.0039141435785699;
-0.0097281013561957; 0.0005995823019719; -0.0268692907533537; 0.0427947343477884; -0.00435672330153435; -0.0152466878370042;
-0.0573331595664285; 0.0328032910930738; 0.0251850818666038; -0.0260102112489004; -0.0243041554069015; 0.0022419377375543;
0.0381379276470177; 0.0209648119836023; -0.0208999350084519; -0.0300157179052307; 0.0464573400794428; -0.0175281161901875;
-0.0104205900475671; 0.0126405168006393; -0.0111013419947575; -0.0220529493496661; 0.0172226163401339; -0.0251335461358406;
-0.0308403449585279; -0.6244514323013870; 0.0826050490502337; 0.0295196078013382; -0.0392965601670690; -0.0088538583391489;
-0.0184152063782218; 0.0139089332651614; -0.0080896718956328; 0.0195268547227861; -0.0243150606664420; -0.0045998164463066;
0.0239801425187895; 0.0214841763653860; 0.0312165068228217; 0.0191368847356257; 0.0251416815929068; 0.0475709449041617;
0.0208986484945460; 0.0066358530042107; 0.0249728000791431; -0.0035878593319943; -0.1232928673839486; -0.0166872704758503;
-0.1597938295311555; 0.0142381308645324; 0.0295316007605039; -0.0014952459795146; 0.0499960839899375; 0.0096862417717702;
-0.0071060931646517; -0.0092052397078608; -0.0206180538482014; -0.0198218350926467; 0.0118433768172123; 0.0130357803758576;
0.0253033261502949; -0.0042411491703653; 0.0217373252198635; 0.0041005030723602; -0.0317700266628011; -0.0373467593763700;
0.0464942047453784; 0.0135199487053068; 0.0108068556982956; 0.1085350617270592; -0.0101490028439339; -0.0975473264082280;
0.0175671081675555; 0.0449399183919388; -0.0122025727429490; 0.0167473025791020; 0.0568635880124885; 0.0548082857971509;
-0.0138902968787213; 0.0250257712159928; 0.0309549079243438; 0.0224810794410547; -0.0039934955241769; -0.0113590512428575;
-0.0230632599836814; -0.0265566814215679; 0.0044107748536554; 0.0021292203354744; -0.0285826450460710; 0.0802106796370616;
-0.0181964791036453; -0.0223373634252233; 0.0162523683640703; -0.0227290545593660; 0.0411945683321473; 0.0165781852465428;
-0.0575450881113194; 0.0239330291674368; 0.0193153774192964; 0.0448165651542644; 0.0480792450332562; 0.0097708065083441;
-0.0035389627709702; -0.0077644058073897; -0.0281290555573772; 0.0095058873045372; 0.0127800708284074; -0.0173047475199783;
-0.0507283355760035; 0.0111752644855045; -0.0123561066100708; 0.0133503687677549; -0.0087753881781146; 0.0061697693806032;
```

Fig. 6. Initial data for a 300-dimension vector of each time frame

In Case II, the Scraper program processed data when one worker and 2 threads were activated.

In Case III, the Scraper program processed data when one worker and 4 threads were involved.

The studies showed the program to expedite (Table 1).

The developed Skraper program allowed obtaining information with respect to the dynamics of the word number on news websites of a certain frequency, i.e., of the time frame required, and using them in the future, with certain patterns being revealed. Using "Word2vec," the obtained data generated a 300-dimension vector.

The vectors representation is known to be a general name for various approaches to modeling a language and representation learning in natural language processing that is aimed at matching words (phrases) in certain vector vocabularies and reducing the number of words. The theoretical basis for the vector representation is the distributional semantics [7].

There are several techniques for constructing vectors. For this purpose, there are neural networks—a dimensionality reduction technique over word co-occurrence matrices and explicit representations trained on word contexts.

Table 1. Expedition effect

Worker configuration	Execution time, sec	Expedition
1 worker and 1 thread	25.70	–
1 worker and 2 threads	19.70	1.30
1 worker and 4 threads	18.04	1.42

It is important to understand how vector representations of words are obtained in the word2vec algorithms. The word vectors are known to be the basis for many natural language processing (NLP) systems that have conquered the modern world (Amazon Alexa, Google translate, etc.). Word vectors are numerical representations of words that preserve a semantic connection between them.

For example, for the vector *cat*, one of the closest words is *dog*. However, the vector representation of the word *pencil* is quite different from the *cat* vector. This similarity is related to the frequency of the two words (i.e. [cat, dog] or [cat, pencil]) in one context). The Word2vec algorithms use a context to generate numerical representations of words, so words used in the same context have similar vectors.

Vectorization makes it possible to show semantically similar words in close vectors of a certain model, while words that are far in their meanings look different. This is the desired model's property that can give a better result.

To train word sampling without pre-marked data, some problems were to be solved, i.e. to create format data tuples and a model that receives one-hot vectors at input and output, as well as determine the loss function and model performance.

It was also necessary to create structured data from the initial text. For example, *The cat pushed the glass off the table.*

Data of the required format were obtained as follows. Each of the brackets indicates a single contextual window. The blue field indicates the input one-hot vector (target word) and the red field indicates the output one-hot vector (any word in the context window except for the target word). Two data elements are obtained from one context window (two neighboring ones are generated per a target word). The window size is usually user-defined (Fig. 7).

The information obtained in the vector representation can be further used in special applications that allow the generation of text reports in neural network ROB advisors and convolutional neural networks (CNN and TCN) to recognize signals of new innovative and technological trends. Being a technology that is based on distribution semantics and vector representation of words, the Word2vec is a set of models to analyze semantics of natural languages.

In our study, signals were generated after processing words retrieved from news sites and "packed" as datasets. The words that appeared in the news for a quarter were counted; their numerical values were summed up quarterly for a certain period. It was

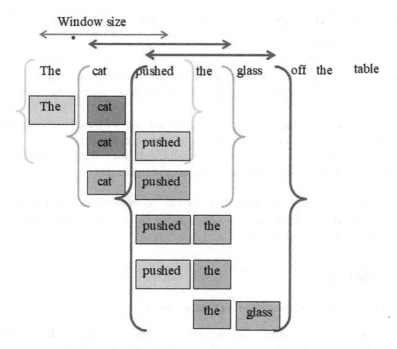

Fig. 7. Structured data created from initial text [7]

important to identify the "spike"-words, whose parameters exceeded the median values. All "spike"-words fell into the list. Associating the information received, namely, frequency deviations, with the data mined by the Skraper program developed by the authors allowed us to assign the corresponding "frequency indices" of information in terms on certain startups and investment projects; their list was generated and is constantly updated. Tracking the dynamics of the changing vectors enabled obtaining information on emerging innovative and technological trends.

The information of that kind could be indirectly used to calculate the global innovation index (GII). The evidence from practice shows that the Russian global innovation index is not great. Russia is ranked 45th in the GII.

It is not difficult to create an integration index for any country in the world that would reflect the level of rapid development resulted from the recent advanced innovations implemented. The index could be useful in developing innovative strategies and policies in order to increase their technological and innovative competitiveness and identify innovative and attractive research areas at the stage of their inception, which will provide a powerful competitive edge that can ensure leadership in one or another field of research.

Monitoring the dynamics of information on innovations implemented by companies and start-ups makes it possible to draw important conclusions and allow correct adjusting the innovation policy of organizations and states. It is no coincidence that the "May decrees," radically changing the vector of innovative and technological development of the state, were adopted in Russia.

1.3 Innovative Technologies and Trends in Dynamics

Innovative trends in economic and financial spheres are:

– robotic process automation (RPA) that considerably helps organizations;
– the global RPA market grows by about 30% annually, its volume reached $ 2.3 billion in 2019;
– transformation of information systems: machine learning tools used at the corporation sare being transformed and implemented on a commercial scale;
– and business analysis tools are being transformed "from detail to alert "due to automated tools that warn people about events and trends that require their attention.

According to Thomas Friedman, who wrote the book "The world is flat", the main global trends in innovation and technology are venture capital investments in IT, biomedicine, and "clean technologies".

2 Methodology

2.1 Analysis and Constructing of a Dynamic Model

The research applied monographic and analytical methods, artificial intelligence, design and construction, some approaches used in Hadoop, and capabilities available in the Deductor platform, in particular, data quantization, Kohonen map, as well as analysis, modeling, study, and generalization.

In order to generate a model, we used statistical data, reflecting the development of the economic sphere and the financial sector of Russia quarterly for the period of from 2015 to 2018, as well as individual parameters the global economy, including the US dollar and VIX-Index.

3 Results and Discussion

3.1 Quantization of Big Data by a Neural Network

Artificial intelligence systems are growing rapidly. They represent an increment of scientific approaches described in scientific works, for instance, new delay-dependent stability criteria for recurrent neural networks with time-varying delays [9] (Bin Yanga and Georgi M. Dimirovskie 2015).

Our neural network model includes the following parameters: GDP (billion RUB), Key rate (%), RTS index, Innovation output (billion RUB), innovation costs (billion RUB), dollar exchange rate (RUB), net profit (billion RUB), risk (σ), loans granted (billion RUB), VIX-Index, and forecast of the volume of innovative products (billion RUB). The model was based on the approaches developed earlier by N.I. Lomakin [1], who used artificial intelligence systems to improve monetary policy.

The baseline data under consideration are presented in Table 2.

The VIX option dynamics is presented below (Fig. 8). The Chicago Option Exchange volatility index—better known as "VIX"—is the most accurate market tool for evaluating

Table 2. Baseline data (a fragment)

Quarter, year	GDR, billion RUB	Key rate, %	RTS index	Innovative products, billion RUB	VIX-index	Volume of innovative products predicted, billion RUB
Q1, (from 23.03/18)	15569.6	7.25	1261.4	852	17.86	852
From 12.02.18	15569.6	7.5	1261.4	850	25.61	850
Q4, (8.12.17)	92037.2	7.75	1154	3403.1	9.53	3403.1
From 30.10.17	61358.1	8.25	1113	2552.3	10.18	2552.3
Q3, (18.09.17)	61358.1	8.5	1136	2552.3	10.15	2552.3
Q2, (From 19.06.17)	46018.6	9	1001	1701	10.37	1701
From 02.05.17	30679	9.25	1053	1701	10.59	1701
Q1, (From 27.03.17)	15339.5	9.75	1113	850.8	12.5	850.8
Q4, 2016	86148.6	9.75	1113	3723.6	14.04	3723.6
Q3, (19.09.16)	64611.5	10	991	1792.7	15.53	1792.7
Q2, (14.06.16)	43074.3	10.5	931	1861.8	20.5	1861.8
Q1, 2016	21537.15	10.5	931	930.9	13.56	930.9
Q4, 2015	83387.2	10.5	931	3258.2	18.21	3258.2
Q3, (03.08.15)	62540.4	11	833	2443.6	12.56	2443.6
Q2, 2015	41693.6	11	833	1629.1	15.39	1629.1

expected volatility calculated using on-line bid/ask quotes for S&P 500® Index (SPX) options.

The VIX evaluates close-to-expiration (more than 8 days) options and determines the coefficient that is a value of the index volatility expected on the S&P 500 over the next 30 days.

In order to predict the volume of innovative products, an XL-file was generated with the initial statistical quarterly data for Russia for the period of 2015–2018, namely, GDP, billion RUB; Key rate, %; RTS Index; Innovative products, billion RUB; Costs

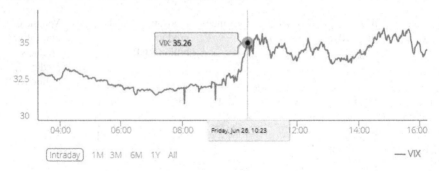

Fig. 8. VIX option

for innovations, billion RUB; UDS, RUB; Net Profit, billion RUB; Sigma risk; Loans granted, billion RUB; and volume of innovation products predicted, billion RUB.

The XL-file was imported into the Deductor program for further processing; the data were quantized. The results are presented below (Table 3).

Quantization is splitting a range of allowed values into a finite number of levels, with subsequent rounding these values to the levels closest to them.

The relationships between the considered factors can be seen in the multidimensional diagram below (Fig. 9).

The quantization results served as the basis for subsequent visualization of big data due to a multidimensional diagram. In the Russia's GDP dynamics, there was identified a trend, depending on the cost of innovations produced in the country and stock quotes of the VIX option in the global economic landscape. For example, the country's GDP increased in the range from 21537.15 to 83.387.2 with an increase in the cost of innovations produced in the country from 930.9 to 2443.0.

It should be taken into account, that the greater was the growth rate of the GDP graph, the lower was the VIX index. In particular, the VIX index from 18.21 of the GDP value did not exceed the value of 61,368.1, while the VIX index in the range of 15.39–18.21 corresponded to the maximum GDP parameter, since it lied within the range of 61358.1–83.378.2 billion RUB.

3.2 Innovative Products Predicted by Neural Network

The developed AI-system allowed forecasting the cost of innovative products, using the "what-if" function in the Deductor platform.

The "what-if" function in the Deductor platform enabled calculating values of the output parameter "Prediction of the volume of Innovative products" (Table 4).

According to the output data of the model, the value predicted for the parameter of the volume of innovative products for the next quarter was 853 billion RUB.

Domestic experience indicated that artificial intelligence systems are widely used for solving practical problems in large enterprises, banks, and IT companies.

Table 3. Data quantized by Deductor (a fragment)

Quarter, year	GDR, billion RUB	Key rate, %	Innovative products, billion RUB	VIX-index	Volume of innovative products predicted, billion RUB
Q1, (from 23.03/18)	Before 21537.15	Before 8.25	From 636 Before 735.7	From 15.39 Before 18.21	Before 930.9
From 12.02.18	Before 21537.15	Before 8.25	Before 367.8	From 18.21	Before 930.9
Q4, (8.12.17)	From 83387.2	Before 8.25	From 735.7	Before 10.37	From 3258.2
From 30.10.17	From 61358.1 Before 83387.2	From 8.25 Before 9.25	From 636 Before 735.7	Before 10.37	From 2443.6 Before 3258.2
Q3, (18.09.17)	From 61358.1 Before 83387.2	From 8.25 Before 9.25	From 636 Before 735.7	Before 10.37	From 2443.6 Before 3258.2
Q2, (From 19.06.17)	From 43074.3 Before 61358.1	From 8.25 Before 9.25	From 424 Before 636	From 10.37 Before 12.56	From 1701 Before 2443.6
From 02.05.17	From 21537.1 Before 43074.3	From 9.25 Before 10	From 424 Before 636	From 10.37 Before 12.56	From 1701 Before 2443.6
Q1, (From 27.03.17)	Before 21537.15	From 9.25 Before 10	Before 367.8	From 10.37 Before 12.56	Before 930.9
Q4, 2016	From 83387.2	From 9.25 Before 10	From 735.7	From 12.56 Before 15.39	From 3258.2
Q3, (19.09.16)	From 61358.1 Before 83387.2	From 10 Before 10.5	From 424 Before 636	From 15.39 Before 18.21	From 1701 Before 2443.6
Q2, (14.06.16)	From 43074.3 Before 61358.1	Before 10.5	From 367.8 Before 424	Before 18.21	From 1701 Before 2443.6
Q1, 2016	From 21537.1 Before 43074.3	Before 10.5	Before 367.8	From 12.56 Before 15.39	From 930.9 Before 1701
Q4, 2015	From 83387.2	Before 10.5	From 735.7	From 18.21	From 3258.2
Q3, (03.08.15)	From 61358.1 Before 83387.2	Before 10.5	From 424 Before 636	From 12.56 Before 18.21	From 2443.6 Before 3258.2
Q2, 2015	From 21537.1 Before 43074.3	Before 10.5	From 367.8 Before 424	From 15.39 Before 18.21	From 930.9 Before 1701

It should be noted that the level of digital innovations is a rather low in Russia compared with developed countries. In order to fundamentally change the situation, relevant regulation documents were issued in Russia in May 2017. Their purpose was to stimulate organizations to actively digitalize all functional areas of their activities.

3.3 Discussion

Overseas experience showed that the largest global companies, such as IBM, Google, and Facebook, are trying to overtake each other in terms of AI. The giants such as MDC, Huge, Group M, and Team One are increasing the chat bots production. The global market dynamics of smart machines—hardware and software systems—amazes with its powerful growth. According to experts, the market for artificial intelligence systems and Internet of things will increase from 7.4 billion dollars in 2019 to about 15 billion dollars in 2021.

It seems advisable to use some trends of the overseas AI development in Russia. For example, according to analyst Forrester Duncan Jones, more and more software

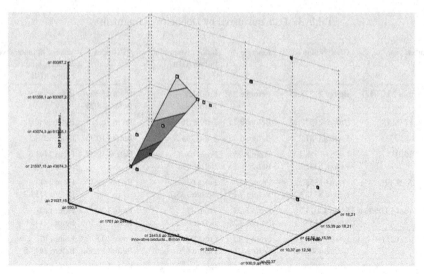

Fig. 9. The GDP trend, depending on the cost of innovative products and VIX option investments

Table 4. Neural network forecast of the cost of innovative products determined with "what-if" function in the Deductor platform

Parameter	Value
Input	
GDR, billion RUB	15569.6
Key rate, %	7.25
RTS index	1261.44
Innovative products, billion RUB	852
Costs for Innovations, billion RUB	702
USD, RUB	57.1658
Net profit, billion RUB	2.5
Risk (σ),	2.8
Loans issued, billion RUB	31567.6
VIX-Index	17.86
Output	
Volume of innovative products predicted, billion RUB	852

providers will embed artificial intelligence into their products, reducing the need for IT services. "In the end, you will manage by exceptions, not standards," Jones said. "This is my forecast for business software. Processes will be performed manually to a much lesser extent. Everything will be debugged and automated, so that people will be able to observe what really requires control, and the program will cope with everything else".

Analytical TAdviser Center conducted a study "Corporate Venture in the IT industry in Russia, 2016–2018." As part of the study, an attempt was made to systemize the corporate venture capital market in the Russian Federation in a segment related to the information technology industry and digital business. There was noted the RF leadership's initiative on the state corporations' higher priority of special units and venture funds that invest in small innovative companies of corporate venture funds.

To identify innovative trends, the Ministry of Economic Development and Trade proposed a large package of measures. There is a need to create a regulatory framework, primarily in terms of technological standards and technical regulation. Of great importance is the organization of work to create a network community in Russia, since several thousand companies of that kind have no communication. It is important to rebuild financial instruments to promote demand for technological innovations and support start-ups by domestic grants, since a considerable share of business that really matters on the IT market of Russia are companies partially owned by the government.

Experts noted problems in the interaction between the IT-market players, as well as a discrepancy between the trend assessment and dynamics of the domestic innovations. For example, the Russian Venture Capital Association (RVCA) described the venture capital activity for 2018,included only the data on corporate venture funds in its statistics, without the term "corporate fund" being specified, and recorded only four transactions in the amount of 6 million US dollars and two "yields" in 2016; three transactions of 7 million US dollars in 2017; and not a single transaction in 2018, with 100% of these transactions being in the sector of "information communications and technologies".

The latest National Report on Innovations (released in July 2018) was prepared by the Russian Venture Company for the RF Government, covered only 2017, and in part about corporate activity fully referred to the RAVI analysis given above. In contrast, the joint RVC and IncRussia study (released on September 28, 2018) counted 24 transactions in the corporate segment for a total of 5,517.7 million RUB, with many transactions consummated not in the IT and telecommunications sector, but in related or other sectors. For example, the CityMobil online taxi fleet purchased by the Mail.ru and Megafon group was considered the largest transaction for the period. Thus, there is a clear lack of objective and consistent information.

Domestic experience is important for the world science, since widely used digital technologies will enable the network interaction between the participants of the innovation process. The search for innovation trends is one of the priorities in Russia, since they allow identifying growth vectors and buying promising start-ups, which results in technological transformations to get competitive advantages, optimize the use of economic and other types of resources, and increase interaction and coordination.

There are more than 40 Google's projects today. They include both mass-use services, i.e. search, Drive, Photos, Maps, Plus, Play, and Youtube, and more specialized tools—API for developers and web analytics tools. Google traditionally maintains its geek-image, so the projects like lunar maps, AR-game Ingress, or semi-secret Google X with its futuristic developments appear every now and then.

Facebook—another giant that loves to buy technology teams—has the total amount of transactions of slightly above $ 23 billion.

Obviously, today Google is striving "in spurts" and purchases ready-made teams to develop two directions.

The first one is cartography. The company is here an undisputed world leader, though certain stagnation in the technology has been observed. The fact that Google purchased Skybox Imagine and launched resonant promo maps of the Moon and Mars surfacese videnced that the company has not lost its interest in this direction.

The second direction is the IoT, the smart home concept. Since Nest was purchased, Google has had no advanced progress in this direction; the acquisition of Drop cam served as a timely investment into the technological boiler.

According to a study conducted by the CB Insights, projects in nine countries, i.e., the United States, China, France, Israel, Spain, Canada, Taiwan, Japan, and the United Kingdom, made 100 most promising AI start-ups.

The USA dominated and had 76 projects. China had eight start-ups, with four of them being in the top ten, and was ranked 2nd. In terms of the amount of investments invited, China held the leading position, because 46.7% of all the money was received by the start-ups of the Middle Kingdom. It is curious that American funds are actively investing in Chinese projects. If you pay attention to the subject field, the study primarily revealed the problem areas of the United States, i.e., 11 start-ups were in the field of cybersecurity, eight projects in health care, and seven companies in enterprise applications. The data protection, countering cyber attacks, unsolved problems in health care, automation of production, and business processes are topical for the United States.

China is actively fighting for leading positions in the media space. Byte Dance claims to be a top corporation. China also seeks to catch up with the leaders of the Fourth Industrial Revolution and has digitized enterprises, offices, and service sector. A marker for this trend is strong Chinese inter-industry AI projects and robotics start-ups.

The digital Hadoop and Deductor AI-system proposed to support management decision-making in studying innovative trends and the VIX option dynamics in the global economic landscape is a kind of "first step" on the way to modeling the development and growth of Russia, with the risk accumulated in the investors' "VIX fear-index" being considered.

This approach is important to find the optimal development trajectory of the country as a certain "smart organism" and allows for objectivity and global results of big data processing, eliminating bias and subjectivism of individual experts.

Creating a more perfect AI system could be the next step of work. Today, the artificial intelligence may be entrusted with some business tasks, i.e., to analyze technological and innovative trends on a global scale, select pioneering innovative start-ups in terms of certain criteria, buy them, and thereby provide a competitive advantage, resulting in a rapid growth based on implementing breakthrough technologies, highly-demanded products, and services with high contributed value.

Financing high-tech projects is always venturesome. The most critical deterrent to assess risk of such projects is the lack of a systematic method for this purpose. Sabzian, Kamrani, Mostafa & Hashemi proposed an artificial neural network (ANN) to develop a mechanism for assessing high-tech projects, with risk-related variables and risk assessment index system (RAIS) based on the principal component analysis (PCA) being of great importance.

Current convolutional neural networks (CNN) have achieved impressive performance of computer vision tasks, such as object detection, image recognition, image extraction, etc. Zhuwei Qin, Fuxun Yu, Chenchen Liu & Xiang Chen believe that CNN's deep layers of neural structures are capable to study input functions and optimize an iterative learning process. In order to improve the CNN'sinter pretability, the scientists proposed to apply the CNN visualization that is widely used as a qualitative analysis method, translating internal features into visually perceptible patterns.

In order to establish trust to these models and spread their commercial use, the scientists Tanmayee Narendra, Anush Shankaran, Deepak Vijkerky & Senthil Mani tried to lay the theoretical foundation and used causal relationships to describe the models' general structure for reasoning the CNN [2].

A team of scientists led by Yaya Lee attempted to investigate the mechanism of the synergetic industry evolution based on its convergence and technological progress. They used the self-organization method and Haken model to establish synergetic evolution equations, select technological progress and industry convergence as key variables of the industry evolution system, and use data on patent licensing of Chinese ICT companies [3].

Of great relevance are Russian scientists' investigations related to the AI algorithm based on quantization of big data and intended for trading SiH8 futures contract on MoEx [4]. Prom et al. suggested a perceptron for assessing the performance of students' tasks using bio-data in studying a foreign language in accordance with their competences [5]. Lomakin et al. proposed a neural-network algorithm for assessing project lending for entrepreneurs [6]. Practice of neural networks to study the effect of the RF Central Bank's monetary policy was studied by a group of scientists, including Lomakin, Golodova & Burdyugova [1]. The approach proposed by Petrukhin for automated selection of components in a bearing assembly for diesel engines also deserves considering [14].

The solution is seen in combining the Spark's capabilities (Hadoop etc.) to digitize innovation news and use a convolutional network of deep learning to identify trends, perhaps with "tonality" assessment. It is also necessary to "listen" to the financial market, using parsing of exchanges. This can provide an opportunity to assess financial aspect of the technology trend and result in "BI databases" that are developed with the minimum possible timeframe. These data enable training the CNN-network on the "cat"-"dog" image recognition principle and, if necessary, receiving a "buy" signal. At the next step, the network—a special PR-bot developed—purchases a start-up or gives a command to the stock Rob-bot to purchase the company-developer's shares. For risk hedging, the option portfolios that minimize financial risk due to the Cox-Ross-Rubinstein model can be used.

Among the promising areas of application of the presented scientific development there may be a decision on complexity and complex networks and systems in computational cybernetics [8]. In addition, this may be a decision regarding stability criteria for periodic neural networks with time-varying delays. [9].

The development of modern digital technologies for solving urgent environmental problems [10], as well as the use of neural networks in calculating environmental costs as an indicator of sustainable development, can become a promising direction in the use of neural networks [11].

Among the promising areas of application of artificial intelligence technologies, machine learning, the use of big data are viewed such as: the development of intelligent systems of economic security, financial risk assessment and others.

So, for example, Fedotova G.V. and other co-authors investigated the problems of using the features of the digital transformation of the bank's economic security system [12]. Gontar A. with colleagues studied data mining methods in assessing the level of economic security [13]. Lomakin N.I. with colleagues studied the problem of developing an artificial intelligence system for assessing financial risk due to time series volatility using the GARCH method [14], as well as the problem of assessing financial risk when trading SiU8 futures using a neural network based on the SAR method [15].

Other equally promising areas for the use of modern machine learning systems, deep learning are such as, for example, studies conducted by Dmitrovsky G. Regarding the controller of fuzzy reasoning Petri, reasoning and evaluation of states of Markov chains [16], as well as research on adaptive exponential synchronization of indefinite complex dynamic networks with communication delay [17].

In addition, we should separately dwell on studies regarding the use of artificial intelligence systems in solving problems associated with identifying features of the processes of segmentation and positioning during the construction of an educational brand in the economy of neural networks conducted by A. Kulachinskaya with colleagues [18], also their work on the analysis of the tariff policy on public transport in St. Petersburg [19].

All this certainly confirms the breadth of application possibilities and the ability to serve as a foundation for future research.

4   Program Code

The research study resulted in program codes, i.e., "AI-systems to support management decision-making in identifying innovative trends and VIX option dynamics" and "Quantization-based AI-system to identify Russia's GDP trends, depending on the cost of innovative products and VIX-option stock-exchange quotation." A fragment of the data quantization program (in XML) is presented below (Fig. 10).

The original Kolmogorov's definition that reads "The algorithmic (descriptive) complexity of data sequence is the length of the shortest binary computer program that prints out the sequence and halts," is strikingly compatible to the fundamental theorems of computing languages, grammars, and machines (Turing 1950; Churchland and Sejnowski 1992; Kinber and Smith 2001; Dimirovski 2017).

```
<?xml version="1.0" encoding="UTF-8"?>
<Document>
    <Version>
        <Comments>Аналитическая платформа Deductor</Comments>
        <CompanyName>BaseGroup Labs</CompanyName>
        <FileDescription>Deductor Studio</FileDescription>
        <FileVersion>5.3.0.88</FileVersion>
        <InternalName>Studio</InternalName>
        <LegalCopyright>© BaseGroup Labs 1998-2016</LegalCopyright>
        <LegalTrademarks>BASEGROUP</LegalTrademarks>
        <OriginalFilename>DStudio.exe</OriginalFilename>
        <ProductName>Deductor Academic</ProductName>
        <ProductVersion>5.3</ProductVersion>
    </Version>
    <Properties>
        <Author>HomePC</Author>
        <DisplayName>11111111</DisplayName>
    </Properties>
    <EnvironmentVariables>
        <Version>1</Version>
        <Vars>
            <Count>2</Count>
            <I_0>
                <Name>LocaleID</Name>
                <DataType>dtInteger</DataType>
                <Value>1049</Value>
            </I_0>
            <I_1>
                <Name>DisableFloatExceptions</Name>
                <DataType>dtBoolean</DataType>
```

Fig. 10. Data quantization program script (XML) [Author's development]

5   Conclusions

Based on the study, we can draw the following conclusions.

5.1   Theoretical Foundations

The theoretical foundations for artificial intelligence systems applied in Big Data processing were considered. Comparative analysis of the capabilities of the Hadoop framework and Deductor analytic platform was performed. The technology of mining data from news Web sites, using the developed program Skraper, was presented. There were highlighted some aspects, revealing capabilities of the Word2vec program that was used in the scientific research and provided the vectorization of retrieved words in the format of a 300 dimension vector.

5.2   AI-System for Identifying Innovative Trends

An AI system was proposed for predicting the cost of innovative products of the Russian economy in the conditions of digitalization. There was put forward and proven a hypothesis that the neural network enables forecasting the cost of innovative products in the Russian Federation for the next quarter. The neural network is based on statistical indicators and economic parameters that reflect the dynamics of the financial and economic system in Russia, including the volume of innovative products quarterly for the period from 2015 to 2018.

There was also put forward and proven a hypothesis that a neural network allowspredicting the cost of innovative products in the Russian Federation. The proposed solution is of great practical importance, since the developed AI-system is based on the forecast of the volume of innovative products for the next quarter and provides identification of the economic growth potential. One of the parameters in the model takes into account the dynamics of the VIX option—the "fear index"—that reflects the investment activity in the global economy.

5.3 Quantization-Based AI-System to Identify Russia's GDP Trends, Depending on the Cost of Innovative Products and VIX Option Stock-Exchange Quotation

The developed AI-system is based on the big data quantization and subsequent visualization and, using a multidimensional diagram, makes it possible to identify Russia's GDP trends, depending on the cost of innovative products and VIX option stock-exchange quotation in the global economic landscape.

The quantization-based multidimensional diagram revealed the relationship between the Russian GDP trend and the cost of innovative products accompanied with stock quotation of the VIX option. The developed AI-system allowed forecasting the cost of innovative products, using the "what-if" function in the Deductor platform for the next quarter.

References

1. Lomakin, N.I., Golodova, O.A., Burdyugova, O.M.: Application of neural networks to studying the impact of the Russian central bank's monetary policy. In: Solovev, D.B. (ed.) Proceedings of the International Scientific Conference «Far East Con» (ISCFEC 2018), Vladivostok, Russian Federation, October 2–4, 2018, Far Eastern Federal University, Russia, pp. 1255–1258. Atlantis Press (2019)
2. Tanmayee, N., Anush, S., Deepak, V., Senthil, M.: Explaining deep learning modelsusing causal inference. https://arxiv.org/abs/1811.04376v1
3. Li, Y., Li, Y., Zhao, Y., Wang, F.: Which factor dominates the industry evolution? A synergy analysis based on China's ICT industry. https://arxiv.org/abs/1403.4305
4. Lomakin, N.I., Sazonov, S.P., Onoprienko, Yu.G.: Developing a AI algorithm for trading the SiH8 futures contract at MoEx on the basis of big data quantization. In: Solovev, D.B. (ed.) Proceedings of the International Scientific Conference «Far East Con» (ISCFEC 2018), Vladivostok, Russian Federation, October 2–4 2018, Far Eastern Federal University, Russia, pp. 1250–1254. Atlantis Press (2019)
5. Prom, N.A., Litvinova, E.A., Shokhnekh, A.V., Yovanovich, T.G., Lomakin, N.I.: Perseptron for assessing the students' task performance in learning a foreign language according to the competencies using bi data. IOP Conf. Ser. Mater. Sci. Eng. **483** (2019). The I International Scientific Practical Conference «Breakthrough Technologies and Communications in Industry» (BTCI2018) (Volgograd, Russian Federation, 20–21 November, 2018) / ed. by E.Yu. Malushko, N. L. Shamne; Volgograd State University [et al.]. – [IOP Publishing]. – P. 9
6. Lomakin, N.I., et al.: Certificate of state registration of computer program registration number 2019611182 dated January 23 2019. Russian Federation. Neural network estimation algorithm for project lending for entrepreneurs. VSTU (2019)
7. Word2Vec: how to work with vector words representations. https://neurohive.io/ru/osnovy-data-science/word2vec-vektornye-predstavlenija-slov-dlja-mashinnogo-obuchenija/. Accessed 2 May 2020
8. Dimirovski, G.M.: An overview of fastcinating ideas on complexity and complex networks and systems in computational cybernetics. In: IEEE EUROCON 2017, 6–8 July 2017. R. Macedonia, Ohrid (2017)
9. Yang, B., Wang, R., Shi, P., Dimirovski, G.M.: New delay-dependent stability criteria for recurrent neural networks with time-varying delays. Neurocomputing **151**, 1414–1422 (2015)

10. Shamina, L., Syrneva, E., Kulachinskaya, A.: Possibilities of applying modern digital technologies to solve current environmental issues. In: DEFIN 2020: Proceedings of the III International Scientific and Practical Conference. ACM International Conference Proceeding Series, pp. 1–12 (2020). Article no. 1
11. Egorova, S., Bogdanovich, I., Kistaeva, N., Kulachinskaya, A.: Environmental costs as an indicator of sustainable development. In: International Scientific Conference on Energy, Environmental and Construction Engineering (EECE-2019). E3S Web of Conferences, vol. 140 (2019)
12. Fedotova, G.V., Lomakin, N.I., Tkachenko, D.D., Gontar, A.A.: Peculiarities of digital transformation of the system of bank's economic security. In: Popkova, E.G. (ed.) ISC 2018. LNNS, vol. 57, pp. 1104–1112. Springer, Cham (2019). https://doi.org/10.1007/978-3-030-00102-5_116
13. Gontar, A.A., Lomakin, N.I., Gorbacheva, A.S., Chekrygina, T.A., Tokareva, E.V.: Methods of data intellectual analysis in assessment of economic security level. In: Popkova, E.G. (ed.) Ubiquitous Computing and the Internet of Things: Prerequisites for the Development of ICT. SCI, vol. 826, pp. 455–464. Springer, Cham (2019). https://doi.org/10.1007/978-3-030-13397-9_53
14. Lomakin, N.I., Petrukhin, A.V., Shokhnekh, A.V., Telyatnikova, V.S., Meshcheryakova, Y.V.: AI for assessing financial risk conditioned by the time-series volatility using the GARCH-method. In: Popkova, E.G., Sergi, B.S. (eds.) ISC Conference - Volgograd 2020. AISC, vol. 1100, pp. 747–755. Springer, Cham (2020). https://doi.org/10.1007/978-3-030-39319-9_83
15. Lomakin, N.: Financial risk assessment in the SiU8 futures trading using neural network based on the SAR-method. In: Sukhomlin, V., Zubareva, E. (eds.) Convergent 2018. CCIS, vol. 1140, pp. 156–162. Springer, Cham (2020). https://doi.org/10.1007/978-3-030-37436-5_14
16. Georgi, M.: Dimirovski Fuzzy-Petri-net reasoning supervisory controller and estimating states of markov chain models. Comput. Inform. **24**, 563–576 (2005)
17. Wang, L., Jing, Y., Kong, Z., Dimirovski, G.M.: Adaptive exponential synchronization of uncertain complex dynamical networks with delay coupling. NeuroQuantology **6**(4), 397–404 (2008)
18. Demidova, S., Gusarova, V., Kulachinskaya, A.: Features of segmentation and positioning processes when creating an educational brand in neural network economy. In: ACM International Conference Proceeding Series (2020)
19. Kulachinskaya, A., Yuryevna, K.A., Vitalievna, K.V. Yuryevich, K.Yu.: Analysis of the tariff policy on public transport in St. Petersburg. In: Proceedings of the 30th Conference of the International Business Information Management Association, IBIMA 2017 - Vision 2020: Sustainable Economic Development, Innovation Management and Global Growth (2017)

Industrial, Service and Agricultural Digitalization

Development of the Format of CNI of Regional Food Market Participants Based on Digitalization of Business Processes

Vasilii Kuimov⬡, Eva Shcherbenko⬡, and Liudmila Yushkova$^{(\boxtimes)}$⬡

Siberian Federal University, Krasnoyarsk 660041, Russia
luda210173@mail.ru

Abstract. The dynamics of development of new markets determines the relevance of systemic studies of modern formats of business co-organization, including cooperative network interactions in value chains. The relevance of our study increases when we set the goal of analyzing the role and features of large-scale use of digital technologies in the practice of businesses. Transitioning to cooperative network interactions based on digitalization can significantly change the practices and technologies of functioning, both of individual enterprises, their network associations, and industries as a whole. The article analyzes the trend of the desire of business entities to cooperate in the value chain and the development of cooperative network interactions on the example of the food market. We demonstrate that all small and medium enterprises and households actively use various digital technologies in procurement, sales, relations with the state and business communications. Accelerating all business processes through digitization and computer data processing as a result of basic innovation during post-industrial development creates new opportunities, qualitatively different from the previous ones, and requires significant changes in management, interfirm and interpersonal relationships, policies of states and organizations. Our research confirms the active transition to a new cooperative network type of economy based on digitalization and the leading role of business striving to achieve competitiveness using new tools and resources with the active participation of stakeholders.

Keywords: Food market · Digital transformation · Digital technologies · Cooperative network economy · Multilevel cooperative network interactions

1 Introduction

Existing studies of the processes of change in the activities of advanced innovative enterprises reveal the qualitative aspects of this process. Modern processes of cooperative network interactions (CNI) and the use of digital technologies in small and medium enterprises, especially those not related to the IT industry, almost have not been studied. Thus, processes that are characteristic of the overwhelming majority of business structures remain outside the scope of analysis.

© Springer Nature Switzerland AG 2020
D. Rodionov et al. (Eds.): SPBPU IDE 2019, CCIS 1273, pp. 41–54, 2020.
https://doi.org/10.1007/978-3-030-60080-8_3

Analysis of the processes of business entities' adjustment to new market realities and modern digital technologies in the face of increasing competition, conducted by the authors in recent years, confirms the trends of the formation of new digital solutions and software with fundamentally different properties for business development, as well as significant changes in the practice of interactions of business, community, consumers and the state. This study continues to prove [7–9] that a new type of economy – the economy of new means and resources of competitiveness of businesses, active participation of consumers, public associations and the community as a whole, integrated approaches of public administration and globalization of international practices – is being formed. The authors' studies show that these processes are determined by the desire of businesses to achieve high-quality results in their activities, increase competitiveness in global markets. The possibilities of digital technologies and fast data processing and transfer, the advantages of new communications both within the organization and with partners and customers create new conditions for anticipating consumer requests and quick responses to them, as well as initiate a new co-organization of production, logistics, distribution and retail processes. All this reveals postulates of a new economy – the economy of cooperative network interactions [7]:

- significant variety of goals of organization's activities;
- cooperation with partners, common networking activity, equal partnership for achieving goals of independent activity and the synergy effect;
- integration of interests of society, state, municipalities and business subjects.

According to R. Weiber, new challenges in economics form its new profile, characterized by the following positions:

- in the current market cycle, information dominates economic growth, and digital and computer technology becomes the core of basic innovation;
- integration of labor processes based on technological networks replaces functional specialization based on the division of labor;
- transition to a network economy is provided by telecommunications infrastructure [22, 23].

We can gain new insights from the conclusions of a number of researchers who have long ago noted that scientific and technological progress leads to an increase in labor productivity and to changes in the cost structure, primarily to an increase in the fixed component of costs.

For example, E. Schmalenbach in 1928 concluded that "the growth of the fixed component of costs" will lead to a change in the economic form, the transition from a free economy to a connected one" [17, p. 247]. E. Schmalenbach did not expand on his understanding of a "connected economy". It is known that during this historical period various cooperatives and the cooperative movement as a whole were developing rapidly. This to a certain extent allows us to assume that he foresaw in the future greater interaction and some coordination between businesses to achieve mutual benefits – some elements of cooperative network interactions.

Identified by E. Schmalenbach and confirmed by many researchers, the pattern of growth of fixed costs and reduction of marginal costs significantly affects organization of businesses, among other things encouraging the manufacturer to strive for the rapid sale of the maximum possible volume of products. The most successful maximum sales are achieved in the networks of enterprises forming powerful and widely branched sales structures.

In general, it can be argued that during the last 10–15 years there has occurred an active transition to a new type of economy and social practice due to the efforts of business striving to achieve its competitiveness with new tools and resources. Consumers and their communities are also actively involved in this process, including through social networks. Each of the participants in the modern process of production and consumption of value uses digital technologies.

These claims are supported by a number of large-scale scientific studies and emerging theories: network interactions by M.Yu. Sheresheva [19], transition of hierarchies to the network mode by N.V. Smorodinskaya [20]. A number of well-known scientific schools demonstrate the profound processes of economic change, the basic directions of digital transformation in businesses and the processes of the impact of digitalization on companies: Peter Weill and S.L. Woerner [25]. In these and many other works (Y Pigneur, A. Osterwalder) authors declare the observed trends of modern development – the transformation of businesses under the influence of digital technologies and the change of business models [12]. They note the significant role for business development of cooperation of resources, practices of interactions between businesses, communities and consumers, as well as a change in the role of the state.

According to Edmund S. Phelps, the 2006 Nobel Laureate in Economics, "the modern period is characterized by the continuation of global shifts and the development of new economic and social paradigms that can be described as a transition from a pyramid to a network" [14].

The research described in this publication is aimed at analyzing the connection between the use of digital technologies and the formation of new cooperative network interactions of individual enterprises in local markets. On the example of the food market in the region, where the vast majority of entities belong to micro, small and medium enterprises, the formats of their interactions to achieve common goals are explored. Given the large number, presence of a significant number of small and medium enterprises and households, participants in the production and sales of food products, these studies should demonstrate (or refute) the reality of cooperative network interactions and the use of digital technologies in these primary business structures.

2 Materials and Methods

Accelerating all business processes through digitization and computer data processing as a result of basic innovation during post-industrial development creates new opportunities, qualitatively different from the previous ones, and requires significant changes in management, interfirm and interpersonal relationships, policies of states and organizations. This study confirms the active transition to a new cooperative network type of economy based on digitalization. The leading role in this transition belongs to groups of businesses seeking to achieve competitiveness with new tools and resources and with active participation of stakeholders. According to the results of our study, information and reduction of its costs with innovative orientation based on digital intelligent solutions act as the dominant economic growth source of the modern economy.

In these conditions:

- integration of business processes of technology networks through resource cooperation changes the principles of specialization of functions in the division of labor;
- manufacturer's desire for maximum volumes while reducing the time of marketing of products is determined by the increase in fixed costs and reduction of marginal costs;
- industrial economy takes on informational character, with effects of scale changing network effects;
- the law of diminishing marginal profitability with negative feedback of industrial economy transforms into the law of increasing profitability with a positive feedback in the information one. Competitiveness of businesses considering these new patterns is formed through the development of cooperative network interactions based on digital technologies [5, 6, 9, 14, 15, 20, 21].

Our research is based on the materials of publications of leading scientists who study new forms of interactions of subjects in economics (2010–2020), the influence of digitalization and development of services on formation of new business models: K. Alajoutsijärvi, K. Mannermaa and H.Tikkanen [1], T.S. Baines, H.W. Lightfoot, O. Benedettini and J.M. Kay [2], Oliver Gassmann, Karolin Frankenberger and Michaela Csik, [4], C. Linz, Günter M.-S., A. Zimmermann [11], Dubosson-Torbay, Magali, Alexander Osterwalder, and Yves Pigneur [12], K. Myougnjin, L. Hanku, Y. Hyogun, K. Jee-In, K. HyungSeok [13]. The empirical data of the authors' own research are summarized based on the results of studying the formation of cooperative network formats of businesses, as well as the connection of this process with the development of digital technologies in business practices and the regional economy. The objects of observation during the collection of empirical material based on author's approaches and samples were enterprises and organizations of micro, small and medium sizes in the food market of the region. The basis of the study is a comprehensive method developed by assessing and developing earlier authors' studies, in the aspect of business co-organization for greater competitiveness in the context of globalization, cooperation and enterprise integration (Kuimov 2016–2019) [7, 8], from the perspective of co-competition and co-branding, the phenomenon of collective reputation (Yushkova 2018) [5], in the context of the transformation of marketing technologies (Shcherbenko 2015) [8].

3   Results

The study, conducted since 2014 by the authors, continues to analyze the emergence of new formats of interactions in markets and the role of digital technologies in them. On the basis of a long-term study of these processes in the food market of the Krasnoyarsk territory, it is possible to observe the dynamics of the development and sustainability of indicators that characterize these processes. The basis of observation is the annual selection from the Unified Registry (hereinafter referred to as the registry) of small and medium enterprises and the tax service of the region. The sampling structure of real business entities is determined by their activities and the number of employees. The dynamics of the development of cooperative network interactions between businesses is expressed by the existing long-term cooperation agreements.

Our research shows that there are about 11 000 subjects on the market (Table 1). Their number is virtually unchanged and is not subject to fluctuations, which indicates stability of the food market. Taking into account the specifics of the registry (it is checked no more than two times a year), there is some inertia in the data presented, not exceeding 2% of the sample, which allows us to speak about their reliability.

Table 1. Dynamics of enterprises of the regional food market by areas and cooperative network interactions (2017–2019)*.

Market activities	Microenterprises in the market (including those developing cooperative network interactions)			Cooperative network interactions in small and medium enterprises in the market		
	Number of microenterprises in 2017/ones with CNI, units	Number of microenterprises in 2019/ones with CNI, units	Changes in the number of microenterprises/ total with CNI, %	Number of enterprises with CNI in 2017, units	Number of enterprises with CNI in 2019, units	Changes in the number of network enterprises, %
Production	2326/143	2110/174	−9.3/121,7	101	109	107,9
Recycling	840/312	914/364	8.80/116,6	144	257	178,4
Wholesale trade	1613/14	1584/21	−1,02/150.0	132	138	102,2
Retail trade	3826/216	4520/341	18.1/157,8	108	141	130,5
Catering	1944/123	2206/154	13,47/125.2	143	158	110,4
Total	10549/808	11334/1054	7,44/1130,4	628	803	127,8

* enterprises developing cooperative network interactions were determined by the presence of long-term (1 year or more) relations (contracts) with business partners
* compiled on the basis of authors' own research

Estimation of the parameters of cooperative network interactions is based on the application of the author's method of functional and environmental analysis of V.V. Kuimov [9].

This method develops a matrix approach to the analysis of market processes and involves evaluation of the cooperative network interaction of enterprises emerging in the market by its level, stability, dynamics and development prospects. A significant advantage of the method is the logic of analysis and design of economic relations of the enterprise in an environment producing forces of complex structure and nature of their influence. According to the method, the basic components of a multi-level environment, in which a cooperative network interaction is formed to create value, are: the internal environment (the activities of departments and specific employees), the competitive environment (the experience of competitors and the impact on the enterprise), the environment of partnership interaction (contracting, work to ensure own activities, etc.), social and communication environment (media, contact audiences, communities, etc. in relation to the activities of enterprises) and the global external environment (the influence of legislation, international conventions and working agreements, and individual procedures in the analyzed companies). Detailed evaluation parameters according to the logic of the author's method are assigned based on the following main functions of the activities of the enterprise: adaptive and integrative (AIF, coordination of departments and services of the enterprise to comply with the laws and regulations of the country, constant adaptation to changing conditions), financial and economic (FEF, ensuring financial and economic activity and development), informational and marketing (IMF, analysis of markets and opportunities for development), material and technical support of the enterprise (MTS), human development (HD, working with staff to motivate it and stimulate the development of the enterprise), production and technology (PTF, as part of purchasing, marketing activities, organizing the production process to obtain products or services, and their supply to consumers) [7].

Making the decision of choosing the food market as the object of study is determined by the fact that it is in the sphere of production and sale of food products where small and medium enterprises are more concentrated. A study of their activities allows us to see whether the business described in the theoretical part of the article realizes the main trends in the development of modern markets – cooperative network interactions – and whether it is connected with the use of digital technologies.

Estimates done by the authors demonstrated that the absolute majority of enterprises in the food market of the region studied belong to small and medium categories, and their cooperative network structures manifest themselves as more stable in the market. The number of these structures during the period under study was growing rapidly, by more than 20% annually. Cooperative network interactions of small and medium enterprises in the Krasnoyarsk territory are also developing rapidly: their number has grown by a third.

An analysis of sustainability of development of cooperative network interactions based on measuring the number of enterprises by their product orientation [4, 6] showed that processes of specialization of enterprises are rapidly forming in the market. The number of enterprises engaged in the production of meat, poultry, grain, fish, as well as enterprises in the hospitality industry, is growing. Over the past 4 years, restaurant enterprises have strengthened networking, including through the formation of their own private farms. In the growing segments of the food market, the development of cooperative network interactions between enterprises shows an increase in their number by 3.6%. At the same time, the reduction in the number of enterprises engaged in the production of vegetables and milk is causing concern. On the other hand, the authors note a change in consumer behavior, which has begun to exert a strong influence on the cooperative network interactions of economic agents and the inclusion of the consumer in them. Consumer trends are related to:

- personalization of consumption (healthy lifestyle, religious standards, emphasis on local seasonal products);
- digitalization of search for information about the products and services;
- saving time and reasonable consumption arising from the desire to reduce the costs of searching, purchasing goods, consumption;
- demand for multi-products that solve a range of consumer problems;
- growth of intelligence, consumer awareness, their initiation of the role of a seller.

Consumer trends, in their turn, became a link in the chain of changes of attitude of economic agents towards digital instruments of branding and promotion of businesses.

The presence, increase in quantity (by the purpose of formation) and the development of cooperative network interactions of enterprises in the regional food market reflects the general trends of the modern economy – achieving competitiveness and stability in the markets due to the development of multivariate interaction of enterprises in various business environments and functions. At the same time, the main and large-scale by evaluation parameters (sales, purchases, transportation, cost of services, etc.) interactions are built in the spaces of creating value [7] for each enterprise.

Thus, the results of the conducted analysis show that enterprises developing cooperative network interactions are more stable and strengthen their positions in the market. Among the factors shaping this kind of sustainability, we investigated the use of digital technologies in the activities of enterprises (Table 2).

Table 2. Use of digital technologies in the activities of enterprises in the food market of the region by areas of activity.

	Microenterprises in the market			Small and medium enterprises in the market		
	Number of microenterprises in 2019, units, by areas of activity	Number of microenterprises in 2019 using Internet, mobile networks, other digital technologies, units	Share of enterprises using Internet, mobile networks, other digital technologies, %	Number of enterprises having CNI with partners in 2019, units	Number of network enterprises in 2019 using Internet, mobile networks, other digital technologies, units	Share of enterprises using Internet, mobile networks, other digital technologies, %
Production	2110	1789	84.7	109	101	92.6
Recycling	914	845	92.4	257	241	93.7
Wholesale trade	1584	1345	84.9	138	136	98.5
Retail trade	4520	4126	91.2	141	139	98.5
Catering	2206	987	44.7	158	127	80.3
Total	11275	9092	80.6	803	744	92.6

* compiled on the basis of authors' own research

Table 2 data show that in 2019 the share of enterprises in the regional food market actively using digital technologies has increased significantly. Among them, enterprises involved in cooperative network interactions use them the most systemically in their business processes. The study of the connection between the development of digital technologies and new formats of business co-organization in the form of cooperative network interactions (entrepreneurial networks, cooperatives, etc.) was continued in 2020.

The 2019 study identified a direct proportional dependence on the number of people working in the organization, as shown in Table 3. The results of a simple random observation of the behavior of economic agents of the food market of the Krasnoyarsk territory quite convincingly show that the Internet, mobile communication, social networks are used by almost all participants of the food market. Larger enterprises integrate the entire range of digital technologies into their business processes.

Table 3. The prevalence of use of digital technologies in the activities of food market enterprises, depending on the number of employees, %.

Number of employees, units	Share of market participants using digital technologies, %	Digital technologies in use, %							
		Internet	Mobile apps	Organization website	Legally authentic exchange of electronic documents	Big data	Corporate blockchain	IoT	Cloud storage
Below 10	80–85	80–85	80–85	10	10	–	–	–	–
10 to 20	83–87	83–87	83–87	15	20	–	–	–	10
21 to 50	85–90	85–90	85–90	25	80	–	–	–	10
51 to 100	100	100	100	45	85	–	–	–	20
Over 100	100	100	100	67	100	10	–	–	35

* compiled on the basis of authors' own research

The findings of the survey show that the absolute majority of enterprises have their own website, use software to manage individual business processes, mostly for accounting in procurement, assortment of goods, promotion of products and services, targeting, reputation management in the Internet space, staff time, reporting. All enterprises with a network structure use digital technologies, including in the parent organization, for accounting and analysis of the activities of network branches.

The research has demonstrated that the analyzed organizations mostly used different versions of the 1C software. At the same time, depending on the growth rate of the organization's staff (which, according to our evaluation, is directly related to the scale of tasks solved and income received), the range of the software used increases. So, enterprises with up to 10 and from 10 to 20 employees, mainly use 1C: Document flow, Orders, Mobile client, Mobile cash register. Network enterprises and enterprises with more than 50 employees use mainly the full set of 1C products, including 1C:

Accounting, Salary and Human Resources Management, Trade Management, 1C: ERP Enterprise Management.

The survey shows that the websites of organizations and their use differ significantly in level and function. The mandatory data on all the websites studied were information about the company, its mission, address, phone numbers and contact email address. In all other aspects, the content of these resources was different, and we could not trace the dependence of the site content on the size of the enterprise or its participation in a particular cooperative network interaction. The main content of the organizations' own websites is focused on promoting their products or services.

The author's method of functional and environmental analysis, which was previously mentioned in this article, made it possible to further detail the assessment of the use of digital technologies in the activities of food enterprises in the region, including by functions of interaction with other business entities. This consisted of determining the number of partners of the enterprise's interaction in fulfilling the functions of its activities, as well as the digital technologies used in this process (Table 4) and made it possible to summarize the following conclusions:

Table 4. Digital technologies in use by functions (directions) of activity of organizations of the regional food market in 2019 (number of employees above 100 people).

Function (area of activity of the enterprise)	Digital technologies in use
Adaptive and integrative (AIF)	Internet, legally authentic exchange of electronic documents, mobile apps
Financial and economic (FEF)	Internet, legally authentic exchange of electronic documents, mobile apps, own website, 1C
Informational and marketing (IMF)	Internet, legally authentic exchange of electronic documents, mobile apps, own website, 1C
Material and technical support of the enterprise (MTS)	Internet, legally authentic exchange of electronic documents, mobile apps, 1C
Human resource development (HRD)	Internet, legally authentic exchange of electronic documents, mobile apps, 1C
Production and technology (PTF)	Internet, legally authentic exchange of electronic documents, mobile apps, own website, cloud technologies, 1C

* for the content of functions, please refer to Materials and Methods
* compiled on the basis of authors' own research

- the scale of the organization by the number of its employees does not affect the number of its cooperative network partners. However, when implementing part of the functions, a functionally necessary list of partners is formed for their quality execution. The main interactions within the adaptive and integrative function in the form of constant information communication are carried out with the supervisory bodies. Banks, insurance companies and other financial infrastructure organizations act as partners in the implementation of financial and economic function. Partnerships are formed in the field of information and marketing supply of business with advertising, marketing agencies, which take on the work with the media, the development and maintenance of the company website, its social media accounts, and other work to promote the enterprise and explore its markets. Cooperative relationships and partnerships are also formed in the course of the implementation of the function of working with the human potential of the organization. At the same time, the company forms cooperation with HR agencies, universities and other educational organizations to attract personnel and develop the skills of employees.

- the use of software in the context of enterprise functions characterizes the use of more advanced versions for the implementation of the financial and economic and information and marketing functions, i.e. when dealing with large amounts of information of complex structure and variable dynamics under the influence of many factors. In general, however, microenterprises, small and medium enterprises in the regional food market predominantly use standard and widespread computer programs (1C, 1C: Human Resources, 1C: Document Flow, etc.).

- the ability to process and transmit data quickly, the benefits of digital communications within the organization, as well as with partners and customers, create new conditions for anticipating consumer requests, responding quickly to them, and initiate a new co-organization of production, logistics, distribution and retail processes. The large-scale use of modern software and digital tools for situation analysis and decision-making accompanies the implementation of procurement, marketing and production and technology functions of enterprises with a wide range of business partners. For large enterprises, several thousand different organizations can act as procurement partners. Software products of end-to-end technologies and state-of-the-art digital solutions (corporate blockchain, cloud storage and processing of big data, legally authentic exchange of electronic documents, etc.) are used to effectively manage cooperation of this scale.

The results of this study, conducted on the food market of one of the characteristic regions of Russia, give a clear idea that its entities (micro, small, medium enterprises and households) are more and more aware of the new opportunities for achieving quality results through interactions with other business entities. A significant part of such interactions is built on the basic principles of cooperative network interactions, including: recognition of the development goals agreed upon, cooperation of resources or their parts, independence and initiative of all participants, compliance with generally unwritten rules of interaction within the interaction. In recent years, state cooperative support programs in Russia have also contributed to this development.

A qualitatively new stage in the food markets of the region may be the adopted program for the development of the local economy, implemented in the region under study. The main goal of this program is to build using the resources of local authorities (in districts and councils), based on established conditions and presence of real potential entrepreneurial structures, their cooperative network interactions in value chains, from the production of products, through their processing to sales in retail and catering.

In the concept of this program, the municipal integrated development projects (MIDP) of the corresponding territory become the mechanism for implementing cooperative network interactions. Initiative businesses and local government represented by the municipality and/or village council can apply for such a project. In the already developed and implemented projects, the "core of the project," the main initiators of interactions in the formation of the value proposition and investors in development of this territory, is particularly distinguished. Among them, as our preliminary surveys show, are primarily medium-sized businesses, including OJSC, LLC, large businesses of individual entrepreneurs. In addition, the program provides for the formation of value-added cooperatives with the participation of farms and households. Relations between them are built on the basis of some principles of cooperative network interactions, including recognition of development goals, some cooperation of resources and constant discussion of the results of this kind of partnership. It is important that the departments and services of municipalities become centers of consultation and formation of a digital space for the exchange of information between participants of the MIDP.

The basic principles of such activities are included in the program document for the development of the studied region – "Development strategy of the districts of the region until 2030". Thus, the formation and development of cooperative network interactions of business entities have become a beacon in the activities of local authorities of the territories (districts) of the region. It is also important that the budget of the region and local budgets of its districts provide funds to support such municipal integrated development projects. In addition, our studies have shown that, in general, all participants in the food market have opportunities, cooperation practices, and are also increasing their experience in using digital technologies in their businesses. All this allows us to draw conclusions about the prospects of development and surfaces a new qualitative stage in the formation of cooperative network interactions at the primary level of production and settlement relations.

4 Discussion

Research into the practices of business entities in their quest to achieve competitiveness with new tools and resources and the active role of consumers and communities in this process, as well as changes in the activities of enterprises in connection with the introduction of digital solutions, defines the leading areas of these processes:

- active transformation of business processes and business products in line with consumer needs and prioritizing working with consumers (customers);
- using state-of-the-art software and digital solutions and corresponding changes in operational processes of enterprises;
- formation of new business models (including on the basis of digital platforms) and growth of economic efficiency of their cooperative network interactions.

Virtually all the microenterprises, small and medium enterprises in the regional food market under study are using some digital technologies in their activities, most often not as a complex (Internet, organization website, and software according to the area of activity, rarely – a complex of software). After structuring the group of the enterprises studied by the number of employees and industry affiliation, we can see the connection of the processes of digital technology adoption with increased work with customers, changes in business processes, and transformation of business models.

In addition, the role of the state in the process of introducing digital solutions into the practice of business on a systemic basis is growing through the implementation of public policy of digitalization of the economy. It determines the direction and procedure for creating digital platforms for the interaction of enterprises with the tax service, state statistics authorities and social insurance and pension funds, etc., and encourages enterprises to use digital formats for these interactions. The driving force behind transformations in business is the movement of consumer communications with the outside world into the digital space, the active spread of use of mobile applications and other software products in everyday life. Consumer decisions about choosing a product and buying, their trust turn to those businesses that set up the processes of promotion and sales to use digital tools, studying consumer experience.

Other motivating incentives for the active use of digital technologies by enterprises and the development of digital solutions to their interactions are:

- digitalization of activities of business partners in the supporting infrastructure: financial, insurance, transport companies, wholesale and logistics centers, communications, suppliers of electricity, water and other life-supporting resources and their transition to digital formats for servicing enterprises;
- digitalization of the provision of state and municipal services, including procedures for permitting land allotment, issuing licenses, various kinds of approval, etc.

However, together with these positive development trends, we should take into account the frequent liquidation and resumption of activities of enterprises (especially micro and small) in food markets. In addition, many businesses and households are not ready for constructive interaction due to the fear of losing independence, and often their business as a whole. At the same time, an analysis of modern legislation shows that the practices of the courts, antitrust and tax services do not take into account new trends in cooperative network interactions in their activities, often hindering their development. Similarly, banking systems and budgetary support for the development of small and medium-sized businesses practically do not create conditions for qualitative changes in the economy of the food market on its primary level – the production activities of micro, small, medium enterprises and households.

All this requires new comprehensive research, active training of owners of businesses and households, building trust between them and local governments.

5 Conclusion

Our studies confirm the widespread adoption of digital technologies by economic agents of the regional food market. Over the past two years, there has been an increase in application of smart digital technologies by enterprises, the use of their own solutions, tailored to the company's activities, the increase in joint use of digital business models.

The adoption of key digital technologies allows for the comprehensive interaction of all market participants based on agreed goals, resource cooperation, co-competition, but with the preservation of independence and mutually beneficial exchange on a voluntary basis.

New opportunities to obtain big data, the complexity of their interpretation, changes in the role of the consumer and consumer trends direct the efforts of modern business to implement the systemic development of cooperative network structures in value chains, allowing to significantly reduce transaction costs, decrease the timing of projects and get new network effects.

Further research by the authors will be developed in the direction of identifying new opportunities to achieve quality results of enterprises' activities in cooperative network structures, identifying collaborations of economic agents in co-competition formats.

Acknowledgments. The authors would like to extend their gratitude to their colleagues, who have shared their vision during the discussions of the materials of this article, thus solidifying the understanding of the processes and conclusions stated.

References

1. Alajoutsijärvi, K., Mannermaa, K., Tikkanen, H.: Customer relationships and the small software firm: a framework for understanding challenges faced in marketing. Inf. Manag. **37**, 153–159 (2000)
2. Baines, T.S., Lightfoot, H.W., Benedettini, O., Kay, J.M.: The servitization of manufacturing: a review of literature and reflection on future challenges. J. Manuf. Tech. Manage. **20**(5), 547–567 (2009)
3. Vandermerwe, S., Rada, J.: Servitization of business: adding value by adding services. Eur. Manag. J. **6**(4), 314–324 (1988)
4. Gassmann, O., Frankenberger, K., Csik, M.: The business model navigator: 55 models that will revolutionize your business. Pearson, Harlow (2014)
5. Grass, T.P., Yushkova, L.V., Tereshchenko, N.N.: Competitiveness of food markets in Siberia. Innovation Management Excellence through the Vest 2020. In: Proceedings of the 31st International Business Information Management Association Conference (IBIMA), vol. 21, no. 3, pp. 1659–1664 (2018)
6. Komarova, A.I.: Digital economy in Russia: program-legal sources. Creating a society of social justice. Socio-economic aspect, vol. 9(51). Moscow, Russia (2018)
7. Kuimov, V.V.: Economics of Cooperative Network Interactions. Theory. Practice. Opportunities: A Monograph M6 INFRA-M. Moscow, p. 220 (2019)
8. Kuimov, V.V., Suslova, Y.Y., Scherbenko, E.V.: Cooperative-Network Interaction as a Resource of Self-Organization and Achieve Quality Results: A Monograph. NITs Infra-M, Moscow (2019). (in Russian)
9. Kuimov, V.V., Suslova, Y.Y., Scherbenko, E.V., Pankova, L.V.: Marketing Technologies in the Development of Food Markets in the Regions of Siberia: A Monograph. Siberian Federal University, Krasnoyarsk, p. 268 (2015)
10. Kupriyanovsky, V.P., Bulancha, S.A., Chernykh K,Yu., Namiot, D.E., Dobrynin, A.P.: Smart cities as the "capital" of the digital economy. Int. J. Open Inf. Tech. **4**(2), 41–52 (2016). http://injoit.org/index.php/j1/article/view/269/21
11. Linz, C., Günter, M.S., Zimmermann, A.: Radical Business Model Transformation: Gaining the Competitive Edge in a Disruptive World. Kogan Page, London (2017)

12. Dubosson-Torbay, M., Osterwalder, A., Pigneur, Y.: E-business model design, classification, and measurements. Thunderbird Int. Bus. Rev. **44**(1), 5–23 (2002)
13. Myougnjin, K., Hanku, L., Hyogun, Y., Jee-In, K., HyungSeok, K.: IMAV: an intelligent multi-agent model based on cloud computing for resource virtualization. In: 2011 International Conference on Information and Electronics Engineering, IPCSIT, vol. 6, pp. 199–203 (2011)
14. Phelps, E.S.: Mass Flourishing: How Grassroots Innovation Created Jobs, Challenge, and Change, p. 392. Princeton University Press, Princeton (2013)
15. Porth, S.J.: Strategic Management: A Cross-Functional Approach, p. 266. Prentice Hall, Upper Saddle River (2003)
16. Shapiro, C.: Competition policy in the information economy, Foundations of Competition Policy Analysis, vol. 25. In: Hope, E. (ed.). Routledge, Abingdon (2000)
17. Schmalenbach, E.: Die Betriebswirtschaftslehre an der Schwelle der neuen Wirtschaftsverfassung. Zeitschrift für handelswissenschaftliche Forschung. **22**, 241–251 (1928)
18. Shcherbenko, E.V., Kuimov, V.V.: Regional trade as a factor of territorial food market development. J. Siber. Federal Univ. Ser. Human. **10**(12), 1916–1932 (2017)
19. Sheresheva, M.Yu.: Forms of network interaction of companies. I. State University Higher School of Economics, Moscow (2010)
20. Smorodinskaya, N.V.: Globalized Economy: from Hierarchies to the Network Structure, p. 344. IE RAS, Moscow (2015)
21. Chaudary, S.P., van Alstein, M., Parker, J.: Platform revolution: how network markets change the economy - and how to make them work for you. Translated into Russian, edition in Russian, LLC Mann, Ivanov and Ferber, Moscow, p. 440 (2017)
22. Wade, M.R.: The Digital Vortex in 2017 (2017). https://www.imd.org/dbt/articles/digital-vortex-in-2017/
23. Weiber, R.: The empirical laws of a network economy. Prob. Theory Pract. Manage. Int. J. **2**, 67–72 (2003)
24. Weiber, R.: The empirical laws of a network economy. Prob. Manag. Theory Pract. Int. J. **7**, 82–88 (2003)
25. Weill, P., Woerner, S.L.: Becoming better prepared for digital disruption: NACD Directorship 2(April): 2 (2016)
26. Weill, P., Woerner, S.L.: Digital Transformation of Business: Changing the Business Model for a Next-Generation Enterprise, p. 257. Alpina Publishers, Moscow (2019). Translated into Russian

Indicators for Assessing the Development of Smart Sustainable Cities

Svetlana Gutman$^{(\boxtimes)}$ ⓘ and Elena Rytova ⓘ

Peter the Great St. Petersburg Polytechnic University, Saint Petersburg, Russia
SGutman@spbstu.ru, lery@list.ru

Abstract. The article discusses the concept of «smart» sustainable cities providing an overview of the approaches found in various sources. The authors analyze the systems for evaluating smart cities in terms of their digitalization and development. The conducted analysis revealed the similarities and specifics of the Russian and international assessment systems. Based on the analysis of the Russian concept of a «smart city» it was concluded that Moscow is the only successful project to have implemented this concept. The study of the main indicators in Moscow made it possible to single out a number of problems connected with data collection. The authors identified three groups of indicators with varying degrees of compliance with international systems of indicators, accessibility and openness: official statistics in the public domain, data obtained from specialized organizations or in the course of special studies, and data that are not currently available in Russia. The article proposes a strategic map for the implementation of the concept of a «smart» sustainable city that includes the main goals and sub-goals for each of the four components: «Economics and Management», «Quality of Life», «Environment», «Innovation». Based on the experience in implementing the concept of «smart» sustainable cities in Moscow, the indicators that are available and can be used to monitor the development of «smart» sustainable cities in Russia are proposed for each sub-goal. The authors suggest a minimal general set of indicators to monitor the development of the cities that implement the concept of a «smart» sustainable city.

Keywords: Smart cities · Sustainable development · Indicators · Strategic map · ICT · SDGs

1 Introduction

One of the most remarkable and socially significant areas of digitalization in the Russian Federation today is the creation of «smart cities». Since 2019, Russia has been implementing the government's «Smart City» program designed to develop sustainable digital systems based on existing municipalities to improve the efficiency of the city's economy and the standard of living of its citizens [1]. Thanks to information technology, a smart city can implement two important areas of work for the authorities: providing them with the information about the living conditions of the citizens in accordance with their needs; establishing feedback between the administration and the citizens. Smart

© Springer Nature Switzerland AG 2020
D. Rodionov et al. (Eds.): SPBPU IDE 2019, CCIS 1273, pp. 55–73, 2020.
https://doi.org/10.1007/978-3-030-60080-8_4

cities today include Moscow, St. Petersburg, Sochi, Copenhagen, Singapore, Stockholm and Zurich. According to McKinsey research, the number of smart cities on the planet will increase to 600 by 2020.

Cities have always been the centers of social and economic development. People move to cities in the hope of finding a better job and a higher standard of living. At the same time, urban population growth results in a significant burden on the natural environment and limited resources (for example, energy and water) and leads to an increased demand for such services as sanitation, healthcare and education. However, in this case, focusing only on technological solutions and developing a convenient urban environment is not enough to solve the problems of the cities included in the framework of the concept of sustainable development.

The Sustainable Development Strategy of cities as socio-economic systems implies the achievement of Goal 11 (Ensuring the openness, security, resilience and environmental sustainability of cities and towns), put forward in the «Agenda 2015» by the United Nations [2]. The tasks to achieve this goal are primarily aimed at improving the cities environment, accessibility and safety of housing and infrastructure. In turn, these areas affect all constituencies of sustainable urban development: environmental, socio-economic and infrastructural. In the face of the problems caused by rapid urbanization, the authorities are to determine how the urban infrastructure will be developed, how public services will be provided, how citizens will participate in the development of the city, and how all these subsystems will be interconnected. At the same time, the goal is not the convenience, but the transformation of the cities into smart urban environment based on ICT innovations.

Thus, the concept of «smart» sustainable cities allows us to combine development, «smart» convenient technologies, and focus on the environmental and social systems of the city. Sustainable development based on «smart» technologies will make the cities flexible, capable of adaptation, mitigating adverse impacts and stimulating favorable socio-economic and environmental changes.

2   Main Concepts

There are many interpretations of a «smart city» concept. They depend on the level of economic development of the country, on adopted normative acts, standards and regulations, on the initiative of the citizens and their attitude to digital transformations. Let us analyze different definitions found.

A concept of a «smart city» in Russia is not yet legally established. However, the national project under the same name outlines the main goal and five principles underlying the Russian concept of a «smart city». According to the statement of the Ministry of Construction, «smart city is a city convenient for people» [3].

The purpose of this governmental project («Smart City»), to be implemented in the period from 2019 to 2024, is to involve highly qualified specialists to the pilot cities of this project.

The program contains five main principles:

– ensuring comfortable and safe environment;

- focusing on the citizens;
- ensuring the adaptability of urban infrastructure;
- focusing on economic efficiency, including the service component of urban environment;
- improving the quality of urban resource management.

In December 2017, employees of the Research Institute of Technology and Communications identified seven main areas of a digital city.

1. Smart economy
2. Smart management
3. Smart finance
4. Smart infrastructure
5. Smart citizens
6. Smart environment
7. Smart technologies

The "Smart Cities Mission", now held in India on the basis of a hundred pilot cities, does not give a clear definition of a «smart city», saying that it depends on each specific city, its capabilities, resource base and the citizens' initiative. However, the Mission stipulates several basic conditions of the Indian "smart city" [4]:

- uninterrupted supply of water;
- uninterrupted power supply;
- ensuring sanitary conditions, household waste management system;
- effective mobility of citizens;
- affordable housing;
- available ICT and digitalization;
- effective governance, including electronic governance;
- sustainable environment;
- safety of citizens, especially women, children and the elderly;
- education and medicine.

Thus, the Indian «smart city» sets minimum requirements for municipalities with the prospect of new layers of «smartness» in the future. For developing countries, this way of implementing the concept seems most reasonable, as it is impossible to fulfill the conditions of sustainable development without the basic infrastructure.

Deakin and Al-Ouar propose four factors that define the city as «smart»:

1. use of a wide range of electronic and digital technologies;
2. using ICT to transform life and work environment;
3. introduction of ICT technology in government systems;
4. territorialization, which allows for combining ICT and human potential to increase the level of innovation.

Deakin defines a smart city as a city for people who use ICT to meet their needs.

In 2007, Vienna University of Technology defined a smart city as «a city that successfully operates in six areas: mobility, housing, public administration, economics, ecology and population». The rating of «smart cities» is calculated taking into account 90 indicators [5]. So far, the rating has been calculated 4 times - in 2007, 2013, 2014 and 2015. The first three versions rated the cities with the population of 100,000 to 500,000 residents, and the 4.0 version rated smart cities with the population of 300,000 to one million. The general conceptual framework was the same in all ratings, the following areas of urban systems development were evaluated: smart economy, smart government, smart mobility, smart population, smart housing and smart environment.

In May 2017, the international standard ISO/IEC 30182:2017 - «Smart city concept model» was adopted. The standard defined the concept, stating that the main feature of the «smart city» is interoperability, i.e. the ability of elements of the urban system to be functionally compatible [6]. Thus, the International Organization for Standardization defines the «smart city» as a kind of the urban ecosystem based on ICT. The standard is reviewed every 5 years and does not supersede the previous conceptual models described by the Organization related to urban studies.

However, there are other definitions:

«A smart city involves regional competitiveness, transport and information and communication technologies, the economy, natural resources, human and social capital, the quality of life and the participation of citizens in city governance» [7].

«A smart city is a digital technology introduced in all its functions» [8].

Currently, in the scientific community and among politicians there is an increasing awareness of the fact that information and communication technologies (ICT) and their wide application can become the basis for an integrated approach, interconnecting cities as an interconnected network. The goal is to improve the quality of life by combining technological and social innovations and applying ICT to improve the efficiency of such sectors as water management, energy efficiency and transport infrastructure as well as urban safety and waste management. Thus, the concepts of a «smart» and sustainable city merge, as shown in the following definitions:

«The concept is not static, there is no exact definition of a «smart city», but there is a sequence of steps by which cities become more convenient and sustainable, and therefore able to respond more quickly to new challenges» [9].

«The city can be defined as "smart" only when investments in human and social capital, traditional (transport) and modern (ICT) communication infrastructures provide sustainable economic development and high quality of life, with rational management of natural resources through the joint efforts» [10].

«The key features of smart, sustainable cities are the following: sustainability, quality of life, and intelligence. Sustainability refers to such factors as management, environment, climate change and others. Quality of life is associated with financial and emotional well-being. Intelligence reflects an explicit or implicit desire to improve economic, social, and environmental standards, an example of which is "smart" mobility», - said Sehar Kondepudi, Professor of National University of Singapore.

The United Nations International Telecommunication Union's Focus Group on Smart Sustainable Cities has developed a concept for a new term based on the analysis of about a hundred different definitions [11]: «Smart Sustainable City is an innovative city that uses information and communication technologies and other means to improve living standards, efficient activities and services in the cities, as well as their competitiveness, while ensuring the satisfaction of the needs of the present and future generations in economic, social and environmental aspects» [11].

Thus, ICT infrastructure is like the nervous system of a smart sustainable city, which organizes the interaction between its various elements and physical infrastructure. It acts as a basis for efficient functioning of the various smart services.

We can define a «smart» sustainable city as a city in which information and communication technologies allow for the collection and analysis of data to identify and implement technological innovations that can increase the sustainability (socio-economic and environmental) of the urban environment.

3   Literature Review

According to the studies of the UN Telecommunication Union's Focus Group, Smart Sustainable Cities have the following development cycle (Fig. 1):

Fig. 1. The development cycle of a smart sustainable city

Thus, the most important stages in the development of a «smart» sustainable city are the following: the definition of development goals, the development of an adequate system of indicators to assess the goals achievement. At the same time, it should be noted that the development goals involve not only technological, but also economic, social and environmental development. To evaluate the city development, it is necessary to develop new tools for collecting and interpreting arrays of information and work out a system of indicators for assessing the progress in digitalization and sustainability. The indicators will enable the cities to measure their progress over time, compare their results with other cities, share their best practices and set standards for achieving the Sustainable Development Goals (SDGs) at the city level.

There are many systems for evaluating smart cities, their level of digitalization and sustainability. All these approaches are similar but have a number of specific features related to the assessment goals as well as the amount of information analyzed. Let us analyze some international and Russian approaches in the framework of smart cities indicators:

I. Easy park. Smart Cities Index

This index contains many indicators and its focus is on digitalization indicators. A number of indicators are not currently presented in the statistical systems of some countries, including Russia.

II. PwC. Data-driven cities

When forming the index at the first stage of work (semantic and syntactic evaluation of open sources), the analysis of the media and scientific works is carried out on the issues related to smart city technologies. Within this stage, we identify the main issues and key technologies. At the next stage, a comparative analysis and assessment of the readiness of urban ecosystems for the development is carried out according to three groups of indicators: competencies; sources of information; infrastructure. Then, the level of applied information technologies is evaluated in the following areas: transport, utilities, security, the environment, healthcare, etc.

III. National Research Institute for Technology and Communications (NIITS), Smart Cities Indicators

The rating is based on the data obtained from open sources. It takes into account 26 indicators characterizing the level of development of seven key areas of a smart city: smart economy, smart management, smart residents, smart technologies, smart environment, smart infrastructure and smart finance.

IV. The Moscow School of Management «Skolkovo», Digital Life Index of Russian Cities

The digital life index of Skolkovo School of Management is calculated for the 15 largest Russian cities (Moscow, St. Petersburg, Kazan, Volgograd, Novosibirsk, Yekaterinburg,

Nizhny Novgorod, Samara, Chelyabinsk, Omsk, Rostov-on-Don, Ufa, Krasnoyarsk, Perm, Voronezh) and takes into account seven areas of application of digital technologies: transport, finance, trade, healthcare, education, media, public administration. The indicators are selected in such a way as to take into account both demand and supply for digital infrastructure.

V. Key performance indicators for smart sustainable cities to assess the achievement of sustainable development goals. ITU-T Recommendation Y.4903/L.1603 [12]

This KPI set is structured into three main groups: areas, topics, and types. The areas reflect the more general aspects that form the basis for the set of indicators. They correspond to the following three fundamental elements of sustainability: economy, environment, and society and culture. The topic defines a group of specific indicators that describe the area of potential development. Nineteen main topics are identified, and each indicator is related to one specific topic. Some topics include specific subtopics that can be viewed as keywords defining the indicators.

The type of indicator indicates its applicability. In total, two types of indicators are defined: basic indicators that can be used by all cities and additional indicators that can be used by some cities depending on their economic potential, population growth, geographical location, etc. There are some additional indicators that are calculated only for very smart cities. These indicators are optional can be used for self-assessment of the cities.

VI. Standards ISO 37120:2014 and 37151:2015

The standards define a list of targets, the assessment and control of which allows the cities to evaluate their development. ISO 37120:2014 «Sustainable community development. Indicators of urban services and quality of life» governs 46 mandatory and 56 auxiliary indicators in 17 areas.

Standard ISO 37151:2015 «Intelligent infrastructure of public utilities. Principles and requirements for the system of performance indicators» contains a methodology for assessing the performance of smart cities' communal infrastructure in 14 categories of basic community needs (from the point of view of the citizens, leaders and in terms of the environment).

The collection of data from the cities and their analysis is carried out by the international organization World Council City Data (WCCD), which certifies the cities according to ISO standards. Using the standards allows us to quantify the state of different areas in the cities and identify the problem areas. Using data-driven decision-making, the cities can improve their key performance indicators and strengthen their position in the international WCCD registry [13, 14].

4 Sustainable Urban Development Assessment

The assessment of the progress towards the SDGs is a very important tool for cities, as it allows each municipality to have a reference point for its progress both in relation to the Sustainable Development Goals and in relation to other similar cities (in the same country or globally).

In turn, these areas affect all areas of sustainable urban development: environmental, socio-economic and infrastructural. In order to assess the level of sustainability of the cities as socio-economic systems, we should select the factors that relate to all four areas.

SDSN (Sustainable Development Solutions Network) developed the methodology for assessing the compliance with sustainable development goals in the cities of the USA and Italy [15]. In Spain, REDS has also adapted this methodology for its cities [16].

Along with the methodology of SDSN, the World Bank, and others, there are some methods developed in Russia both at the level of large organizations and by individual authors. However, all of the above methods have a complex system of calculations or a large number of indicators that are not supported with the data in the public domain, therefore, they cannot be considered universal and applicable to any city. Since the Spanish organization REDS has the experience in adapting indicators to assess the level of sustainable development of the cities, we will consider it more in detail.

The REDS report methodology, as mentioned earlier, is based on the methodology developed by SDSN for US cities [17], which applies the methodology developed by the Bertelsmann Stiftung Foundation and SDSN for the Global SDG Index [18].

For each of the goals, indicators were identified that allow assessing various aspects of sustainable development and the data from official sources are collected throughout the country at local levels. As a starting point, more than 80 documents on urban assessment methodologies based on urban indicators related to the SDGs were considered. Key reference documents are the following:

- Global indicator framework for the SDG and targets of the 2030 Agenda for Sustainable Development.
- SDG UN indicators SDG Index and Dashboards Report 2017 Global Responsibilities International spillovers in achieving the goals.
- ISO 37120. Sustainable development communities – Indicators for city services and quality of life.
- US cities SDG Index 2017: The U.S. Cities Sustainable Development Goals Index 2017, Achieving a Sustainable Urban America.
- CASBEE for CITIES 2015. Environmental Performance Assessment Tool for Municipalities.
- ITU-T Y.4903/L.1603. KPI for smart sustainable cities to assess the achievement of SDG.
- ICR iCityRate. La classifica delle città intelligenti italiane. Citta e Comunita Sostenibili.
- Sustainable development in the EU. Monitoring report on progress towards the SDGs in a EU context.

5   Comparative Analysis of Indicators of the Sustainable Urban Development Level

To analyze the factors for assessing sustainable urban development, we consider the rating of sustainable cities of Russia (SGM agency), the rating of "25 sustainable cities

Table 1. Comparison of methods for calculating indicators to assess the level of sustainable development of cities used by various organizations [15, 16, 19, 20]

Indicators	SGM	Siemens, KPMG	REDS	UNSDSN
Natural growth rate	+			
Migration rate	+			
Mortality from socially significant diseases	+		+	+
Number of doctors/medical staff	+			+
Number of university students	+		+	
Quality of higher education				+
Number of universities in international academic rankings	+			
Number of recorded crimes	+			
Number of murders	+		+	+
Convenience of housing: heat supply, water supply, sewage systems	+			+
Proportion of families in line for improved housing conditions	+			
Housing renovation	+			
The share of dilapidated housing	+			
Number of casualties in an accident	+			+
Number of Internet users	+		+	
Registered unemployment	+		+	+
Specific pollutant emissions from road transport	+			
Population density	+			
CO2 emissions		+	+	+
Power consumption		+	+	
Average annual heat supply	+			
Number of trips by public transport	+			
Renewable energy consumption		+	+	+
The density of the transport network		+		+
Fixed investment	+			
The proportion of unprofitable organizations	+			
Retail turnover	+			
Waste recycling		+	+	
Urban landscaping policy		+	+	+

(*continued*)

Table 1. (*continued*)

Indicators	SGM	Siemens, KPMG	REDS	UNSDSN
Water consumption per person		+		
Population beyond poverty line				+
Infant mortality			+	+
Life expectancy			+	
Funding social assistance and services			+	
Green farming			+	
Food assistance to disadvantaged people			+	
Food prices			+	
Education funding			+	
Access to Preschool Education Services	+		+	+
Difference in pension payments			+	
Gender pay gap			+	+
Gender violence			+	+
Gender gap in unemployment			+	
Balance of income and expenses in water resources management			+	
Cost of domestic water supply			+	
Energy requirement for residential premises			+	
Balance of electricity and rental costs			+	
The ratio of salaries to the cost of living	+			
Industrial accidents			+	
GDP per capita			+	+
Number of Patents Pending			+	+
Research, Development and Innovation	+		+	
Travel time to work			+	+
Labor integration of persons with disabilities			+	
Labor integration of foreigners			+	
High income concentration			+	
Housing Affordability			+	+
Use of sustainable kinds of transport			+	
Urban vulnerability			+	
Ecosystem productivity			+	

(*continued*)

Table 1. (*continued*)

Indicators	SGM	Siemens, KPMG	REDS	UNSDSN
Flood risk			+	
Relative artificial surface area			+	
Area of protected coastal areas			+	
Money laundering and drug trafficking			+	
Participation in the elections			+	
Juvenile Violence			+	
Collaboration and Development Projects			+	
Integrity and autonomy of municipal institutions			+	
Affiliation with the national networks for sustainable development			+	
Personal income				+
The obesity level				+
Health insurance				+
Normalized Deficiency Index (Water Stress)				+
Gini coefficient			+	+
Absolute Upward Mobility				+
Racial segregation				+
Broadband coverage			+	+

in Spain" developed with the support of Siemens and KPMG, the REDS report "Sustainable Development in 100 Cities of Spain" and the report of UNSDSN "Sustainable Development in 100 US Cities". Some indicators in the analysis were grouped (such as "mortality due to specific diseases" - the general "mortality from socially significant diseases", etc.) or taken into account on the basis of data comparability. The results of the comparative analysis of some indicators used to assess the sustainability of the cities are presented in Table 1.

The most factors used to assess the sustainability of cities in Russia and abroad are different. Nevertheless, the selected methodologies have some common features that can be adapted and used to build the authors' model for assessing the sustainability of socio-economic systems (cities). A brief analysis of the indicators used in different methods is presented in Table 2.

Most indicators used to assess sustainable urban development are also related to other Sustainable Development Goals. Table 3 presents the relationship of factors with the Sustainable Development Goals.

Table 2. The priority degree of indicators for assessing sustainable urban development

	Number of indicators
Indicators used in 3 or more methods	7
The indicators used in two methods	18
Indicators used in one method	52
Total number of the indicators considered	77

Table 3. Matrix for using SDG 11 indicators to measure the progress towards other SDGs

Sustainable Development Goals	SGM	Siemens, KPMG	REDS	UNSDSN
1. Fighting poverty			+	+
2. Famine relief			+	+
3. Good health and well-being	+	+	+	+
4. Quality education	+		+	+
5. Gender equality			+	+
6. Clean water and sanitation	+	+	+	+
7. Low-cost clean energy		+	+	+
8. Decent work and economic growth	+		+	+
9. Industrialization, innovation and infrastructure	+	+	+	+
10. Reduced inequality			+	+
11. Responsible consumption and production	+	+	+	+
12. Fighting climate change	+	+	+	+
13. Conservation of marine ecosystems			+	
14. Conservation of terrestrial ecosystems		+	+	+
15. Peace, justice and effective institutions	+		+	+
16. Partnership for sustainable development			+	+

It can be concluded that both indicators of the cities' sustainability and the cities themselves as socio-economic systems affect the sustainable development of the country as a whole. Table 3 shows that the urban environment largely affects the achievement of the Sustainable Development Goals at the country level, since more than half of the world's population live in cities, and the urbanization level of developed countries exceeds 90%.

Based on the analysis of the tables, we can highlight the most studied indicators of urban sustainability. However, not all indicators can be used in further analysis, since the methods of data collection vary in different countries, and it is not possible to adapt them.

6   Development of a System of Indicators for Analyzing the Level of Sustainable Urban Development

From Table 3, it can be concluded that there are very few identical criteria for sustainable urban development in various methods. Moreover, the listed indicators can be collected in the cities in one country, while they cannot be collected in the cities in another country, or they have different data collection methodologies. Data absence or incompatibility, as well as differences in methodologies complicate the possibility of choosing universal criteria for assessing the sustainable development of cities in different countries. Based on the analysis, the indicators were selected for «smart» sustainable cities (Table 4). Two main criteria form the basis for the selection of indicators: the indicator's compliance with the development goals of «smart sustainable cities» and the use of this indicator in two or more methods for assessing the sustainability of cities.

To monitor and control the implementation of the sustainable smart city concept, the system of indicators and a strategic map for the implementation of the sustainable smart city concept were developed. The strategic map for the development of «smart» sustainable cities is a universal and consistent way of describing the concept of a «smart» sustainable city in which there is an opportunity not only to adjust goals and their corresponding indicators, but also to control the process of achieving these goals. The strategic map reflects causal relationships between individual goals, sub-goals and control indicators. For each control indicator, quantitative threshold values for the development indicators of «smart» sustainable cities were determined on the basis of the data presented in official reports. Thus, the general strategic map presented in the article (Fig. 2),

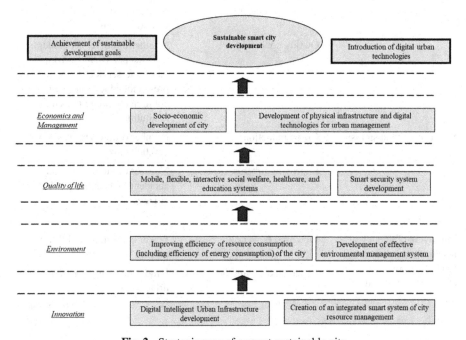

Fig. 2. Strategic map of a smart sustainable city

Table 4. Indicators of «smart» sustainable cities

Goals	Sub-goals	Indicators
Economics and Management		
Development of physical infrastructure and digital technologies for urban management	Urban development	Housing affordability, sq. m per capita Convenience of housing: smart systems of heat supply, water supply and sewage, % of the supplied area of the total housing area
	Urban infrastructure development	Travel time to work, minutes The length of roads, km
Socio-economic development of the city	Urban economy development	GDP per capita, thousand rubles
	Balanced personal incomes	Gini coefficient
	Labor market development	Registered unemployment,% of economically active population
Quality of life		
Mobile, flexible, interactive social security, healthcare, and education systems	Reduced social tension	Mortality from socially significant diseases, cases per 100 citizens Gender-based violence, cases per 10,000 citizens
	Quality healthcare	Number of doctors, doctors per 10,000 citizens
	Quality education	Number of university students, students per 10,000 citizens Access to services in the field of preschool education, % of children attending preschool institutions
Smart security systems	Crime reduction	Number of murders, cases per 100,000 citizens
	Improving urban security	Number of victims in road accidents, casualties per 10,000 citizens
Environment		
Improving efficiency of resource consumption (including power efficiency) of the city	Increased power efficiency	Power consumption, kWh per 1 citizen
	Urban landscaping policy	Landscaping area, % of the urban area

(*continued*)

Table 4. (*continued*)

Goals	Sub-goals	Indicators
Development of effective environmental management systems	Recycling	The volume of recyclables, tons per 1 citizen
	Development of environmental safety monitoring system	CO_2 emissions, thousand tons per year per citizen
Innovation		
Digital Intelligent Urban Infrastructure development	Digital communications development	Number of Internet users, % of the total population
	Digital infrastructure development	Broadband coverage, % of households
Development of an integrated smart system of city resource management	Research, development and innovation in the urban environment	Research and innovation costs, thousand rubles per citizen Number of patents pending, per 10,000 citizens
	Efficient energy management	Renewable energy consumption, % of the total energy consumed

was developed taking into account the features of the development of «smart» sustainable cities. It contributes to the successful implementation of the relevant concept and organization of monitoring performance indicators for specific development tasks of smart cities. The assessment of the implementation of the «smart» city concept starts with the evaluation of its intangible assets, i.e. with its lowest component («Innovation»), then the concrete results at the city level (the top component is «Economics and Management») are evaluated, which provides a holistic assessment of the implementation of the concept. In the framework of individual studies, strategic indicators for each component at all levels of management can be built, from the Russian Federation as a whole to the enterprises of the Russian Federation.

Obviously, it is difficult to determine common approaches to the concept of «smart» sustainable city which would be suitable for all countries and regions. For example, household broadband coverage varies significantly across regions from 15% in Africa to 84% in Europe (Broadband Commission for Sustainable Development). Therefore, on the one hand, it is necessary to establish the values of these indicators based on the characteristics of the country and the macro-region. On the other hand, difficulties arise due to the need of conducting the comparative analysis and using the best worldwide practices. It seems reasonable to create a minimum overall set of indicators that could be monitored and compared across all cities implementing smart sustainable growth strategies. Such a minimal set of indicators is proposed in this paper.

Based on the Russian experience, we can conclude that Moscow is the only successful project to have implemented the concept of a «smart» city. The study of the main indicators in Moscow made it possible to single out a number of problems with the collection of information. Table 5 presents indicators that can be used to analyze the development sustainability for Russian cities:

Table 5. Sustainable urban development indicators [21–26]

Indicators	Data source	Value indicator, 2017
Economics and Management		
Affordability of housing, sq. m per capita	According to the Federal State Statistics Service: Moscow (reference: the maximum value for the cities of the Central Federal District - Bryansk)	19,3 (29,2)
Convenience of housing: smart systems of heat supply, water supply and sewage, % of the supplied area of the total housing area	The indicator is not available in Russia	N/A
Travel time to work, minutes	*According to Superjob.ru, the maximum value for the largest cities in Russia: Moscow (reference: London)	60–70 (90–100)
Length of roads, km	According to the Federal State Statistics Service: the maximum value for Russian cities: Moscow	6 504
GRP per capita, thousand rubles	According to the Federal State Statistics Service: Moscow	1150
Gini coefficient	According to the Federal State Statistics Service: Moscow	0,42
Registered unemployment, % of economically active population	According to the Federal State Statistics Service: the minimum value for Russian cities: Moscow	1,2
Quality of life		
Mortality from socially significant diseases, cases per 10,000 citizens	The indicator is not available in Russia	N/A
Gender-based violence, cases per 10,000 citizens	The indicator is not available in Russia	N/A
Number of doctors, doctors per 10,000 citizens	According to the Federal State Statistics Service: Moscow (the maximum value in the cities of the Central Federal District: Smolensk)	55,9 (99,3)
Number of university students, students per 10,000 citizens	According to the Federal State Statistics Service: the maximum value for Russian cities: Moscow	0,44

(*continued*)

Table 5. (*continued*)

Indicators	Data source	Value indicator, 2017
Access to services in the field of preschool education, supervision and care for children, the number of children in preschool educational programs, % of the number of children of the corresponding age	According to Moscow State Statistics Service	53,3
Number of murders, cases per 100,000 citizens	According to Moscow State Statistics Service	2,5
Number of casualties in road accidents, casualties per 10,000 citizens	**According to the Moscow traffic police	7
Environment		
Power consumption, kWh per 1 citizen per year	According to a PwC study: Moscow (reference: London)	959 (1500)
Landscaping area, sq.m per citizen	*** «Guidelines for the design of residential areas and housing estates of Moscow»	25-30
The volume of recyclables, tons per 1 citizen	The indicator is not available in Russia	N/A
CO_2 emissions, kg per year per 1 citizen	According to Moscow State Statistics Service	0,66
Innovation		
Number of Internet users, % of the total population	According to the Federal State Statistics Service: Moscow (the maximum value in Russian cities: Salekhard)	83,1 (95,5)
The proportion of households with broadband Internet access, % of the total number of households	According to the Federal State Statistics Service: Moscow (the maximum value in Russian cities: Salekhard)	78,1 (93,3)
Research and innovation costs, rub. per citizen	According to the Federal State Statistics Service: the maximum value for Russian cities: Moscow	34059,9
Number of patents granted, per 10,000 citizens	According to the Federal State Statistics Service: the maximum value for Russian cities: Moscow	4–5
Renewable energy consumption, % of the total energy consumed	The indicator is not available in Russia	N/A

In general, three groups of indicators can be distinguished: official statistics in the public domain, data obtained from specialized organizations or in the course of special studies, and data that are not currently available in Russia.

As for the first group of indicators, there are certain difficulties due to the fact that the methodology for collecting information varies in different countries, and even the indicators under the same name may be different, which makes cross-country comparisons difficult.

The third group includes indicators related to the development of new technologies. It also includes new social and environmental indicators that are not yet accepted but closely correspond to the goals of sustainable development.

7 Conclusion

A smart, sustainable city uses ICT infrastructure in a flexible, reliable, scalable, affordable, secure and resilient way to achieve a number of goals. It improves the quality of life of its citizens. It provides a higher standard of living and wider employment opportunities. It improves the welfare of its citizens, the systems of health care, social welfare, physical security and education. It improves services based on physical infrastructure, such as mobility and water supply. It enhances disaster prevention and management, including the ability to mitigate the effects of climate change. It provides effective, balanced regulatory and managerial mechanisms with appropriate strategies.

It can be concluded that a system of indicators for assessing «smart» sustainable cities in Russia has not been developed. Obviously, the set of indicators can vary across countries and regions of one country when the dynamics of each city by its problem points is to be carefully assessed. Thus, a smart city promotes a sustainable approach that meets current needs without affecting the ability to meet the needs of future generations.

Acknowledgements. This research work was supported by the Academic Excellence Project 5–100 pro-posed by Peter the Great St. Petersburg Polytechnic University.

References

1. The Passport of the federal project "Formation of a comfortable urban environment" (approved by the minutes of the meeting of the project committee for the national project "Housing and Urban Environment" dated 21.12.2018 N 3)
2. Sustainable Development Goals. https://www.un.org/sustainabledevelopment/cities/
3. «Smart City» Project Presentation. http://www.minstroyrf.ru/docs/17597/
4. Cities, S.: Mission Statement and Guidelines. Ministry of Urban Development, GoI, pp. 5–7 (2015). http://smartcities.gov.in/upload/uploadfiles/files/SmartCityGuidelines(1).pdf
5. Giffinger, R.: European smart cities: the need for a place related Understanding. In: Conference Creating Smart Cities, Edinburgh Napier University, June 2011
6. ISO: ISO and smart cities (2018b). https://www.iso.org/publication/PUB100423.html. https://www.iso.org/files/live/sites/isoorg/files/store/en/PUB100423.pdf
7. Giffinger, R., Fertner, C., Kramar, H., Kalasek, R., Pichler-Milanović, N., Meijers, E.: Smart cities: ranking of european medium-sized cities. centre of regional science (SRF). Vienna University of Technology, pp. 1–12 (2007)

8. Smart Cities Readiness Guide: The planning manual for building tomorrow's cities today. Smart Cities Council (2015). http://readinessguide.smartcitiescouncil.com
9. BIS: The Smart City Market: Opportunities for the UK (BIS Research Paper № 13). Department for Business, Innovation and Skills, London (2013)
10. Faulkner, D.: Infrastructure for new smart sustainable cities. International Telecommunication Union. Building Tomorrow's Smart Sustainable Cities. ITU News, no. 2. p. 7 (2016). https://www.itu.int/en/itunews/Documents/2016-02/2016_ITUNews02-en.pdf
11. International Telecommunication Union (ITU): Focus Group on Smart Sustainable Cities. https://www.itu.int/ru/ITU-T/focusgroups/ssc/Pages/default.aspx
12. Implementing ITU-T International Standards to Shape Smart Sustainable Cities: The case of Moscow. ITU. 2019.94 C.https://www.itu.int/en/publications/Documents/tsb/2018-U4SSC-Case-of-Moscow-RU/mobile/index.html#p=47
13. Namiot, D.E.: On smart cities standards. Inf. Soc. **2**, 45–52 (2017)
14. World Council on City DataWorld council on city data webpage. (2018). http://www.datafo rcities.org/
15. Espey, J., Dahmm, H., Manderino, L.: Leaving No US City Behind: The US Cities Sustainable Development Goals Index, p. 50. Sustainable Development Solutions Network, Paris (2018)
16. de Madariaga, I.S., GarcíaLópez J., Sisto, R.: MirandoHacia el Futuro: CiudadesSostenibles. Los Objetivos de DesarrolloSostenibleen 100 ciudadesespañolas. Informeurbano. Primeraedición 50 p. (2018)
17. Red Española para el DesarrolloSostenible (REDS). http://reds-sdsn.es/quienes-somos/red-espanola-desarrollo-sostenible
18. Sachs, J., Schmidt-Traub, G., Kroll, C., Durand-Delacre, D., Teksoz, K.: SDG Index and Dashboards Report 2017 (2017). http://www.sdgindex.org/assets/files/2017/2017-SDG-Index-and-DashboardsReport–full.pdf
19. Sustainable Development Ranking for selected Russian cities for 2017. Rating agency SGM. (6), 25 p. (2017)
20. 25 ciudadesespañolassostenibles. Análisis e Investigación (2012). Siemens. KPMG, 68 p.
21. Official website of Rosstat. http://moscow.gks.ru/wps/wcm/connect/rosstat_ts/moscow/ru/sta tistics/. Accessed 05 July 2019
22. Official website of Rosstat. http://www.gks.ru/bgd/regl/b18_14p/Main.htm. Accessed 05 July 2019
23. Official website of Rosstat. http://www.gks.ru/bgd/regl/b18_14t/Main.htm. Accessed 05 July 2019
24. Official website of Rosstat. https://www.mskagency.ru/materials/2751227. Accessed 05 July 2019
25. Research on lost time. Kommersant https://www.kommersant.ru/doc/3306794. Accessed 26 May 2017
26. Gorohov, V.A.: Rationing and placement of green spaces of the city. http://landscape.totala rch.com/node/13

Regional Innovation Systems and Clusters as Drivers of the Economic Growth During the Fourth Industrial Revolution

Accelerating Nation Competitiveness Through Economic Corridor Development: Indonesia Masterplan Revisited

Mohammed Ali Berawi[1]([✉]) [iD], Bambang Susantono[2] [iD], Perdana Miraj[3] [iD],
Mustika Sari[2] [iD], Gunawan Saroji[2] [iD], Abdur Rohim Boy Berawi[2] [iD],
and Humayri Sidqi[2] [iD]

[1] Universitas Indonesia, Depok 16424, Indonesia
maberawi@eng.ui.ac.id
[2] Center for Sustainable Infrastructure Development, Depok 16424, Indonesia
[3] Pancasila University, Jakarta 12640, Indonesia

Abstract. Indonesia has more than seventeen thousand islands grouped into six corridors that span across the country. Considering the steady progress of economic development, evaluation to the national masterplan becomes critical in generating optimum industrial area mapping. The aim of this research is to investigate industrial development by taking into account the characteristics and potential resources in each economic corridor in Indonesia. The research will combine qualitative approach through a desk study, benchmarking, and in-depth interviews to obtain the targeted outputs. The findings of this study show that the priority of industrial development for each corridor is based on its regional potential and competitiveness. The industry types for all the six economic corridors consist of plantation processing industry, ICT industry, natural resources processing industry, aquaculture industry, and tourism industry. This paper also recommend urban and infrastructure development such as road, railway, new IT-based city to support the industrial development in terms of mobility and accessibility for both human and goods.

Keywords: Developing countries · Industrial cluster · Infrastructure · Mapping · Regional development

1 Introduction

Indonesia has more than seventeen thousand islands mostly grouped into six corridors that span across the country. In 2011, the government attempted to generate a national masterplan for economic development namely Masterplan for Acceleration and Expansion of Indonesia's Economic Development 2011–2025 (MP3EI). The document displays economic corridors and its associated industries that should be developed in approximately twenty years. The corridors comprise Sumatera, Java, Kalimantan, Sulawesi, Bali-Nusa Tenggara, and Maluku-Papua. Each corridor has different potentials for development which were based on its natural resources, productivity, human resources, and existing industries.

© Springer Nature Switzerland AG 2020
D. Rodionov et al. (Eds.): SPBPU IDE 2019, CCIS 1273, pp. 77–100, 2020.
https://doi.org/10.1007/978-3-030-60080-8_5

During the past eight years since the MP3EI initiative has been launched, Indonesia experienced a steady growth of economic development. The national gross domestic product (GDP) showed erratic progress started at 6.17% in 2011 then decelerated to 4.88% in 2015 and slowly climbed to 5.17% in 2018. This figure showed that the program in masterplan has limited contribution to the economic expansion of the country.

There are various sectors contributing to the GDP including industry, trade, and construction as the top three sectors that provide 20%, 13% and 11% respectively. As the industry sector generates high economic activities to the nation, the government should pay attention to the industrial cluster and its regional connectivity. It is also believed that increasing the capacity of the industry may have a positive impact on economic activities both at local and national levels [15, 38]. For these reasons, hence an evaluation of the document should be conducted by taking into account the current condition of the nation to come up with a more suitable view to the potential development in each corridor.

This research aims to investigate industrial development by taking into account the potential of each area. The result is expected to generate an alternative concept of industrial development for each of Indonesian economic corridor. The output can be used as an input in developing national public policy and regulation related to industrial focus and regional development.

2   Literature Studies

2.1   Regional Economic Development Theories

Researchers have extensively discussed regional development for these past few decades; however, there is very little consistent understanding on the meaning of region established. As a geographical, territorial or place that can manifest as a state, state, province, district, and village [19]. Region is defined as the hierarchical systems of central cities in central place theory [27, 38], in which each region has both several number of large higher order cities and several number of smaller lower order cities. The order is determined by the goods' diversity and the market area size for various goods. In general, a region is a spatial entity bound to a certain geographic location that consists of many connected parts, which have impact on each other due to various activities such as the flow of people, economy forces, social culture, and local resources. This space has unique characteristics and goals, but still interconnected and influential with others [11].

The regional development cannot be separated from economic development because the economic activity growth is supported by the existence of an area, which is the baseline for conducting any economic activities. There are several basic theories on regional development related to the economic development, including interregional convergence hypothesis extended from neoclassical trade theory, which was further experienced advances and improvement to location theory, central place theory, and regional science.

Most of the initial theories related to the development of regional economy started with the neoclassical theories on the national economic growth and international trade [13]. The neoclassical theory simultaneously foresees that the discrepancies in labor prices and other factors throughout the regions will decrease and tend toward convergence in the long run [29]. Over time, a region can be categorized as a developed area based on per capita income from industries that it owned [17], a thesis that proposes a promising standpoint for poor regions [14]. This theory assumes that the rate of national growth is the total of individual regions' growth rates, therefore, the rate of national economic development can be increase by achieving growth in a particular region. Growth models of neoclassical theory are characterized by three core assumptions, namely the predetermined level of technology, the production function that shows constant returns to scale in the production factors for a constant level of technology, and the factors of production that have diminishing marginal products [20].

The theory of regional economic development has been through several stages of change. As a respond to the false rejection that people did not consider the region's condition in conducting economic analysis, location theory was developed consequently by several theories namely Weber in 1929, Hover in 1937, Greenhut in 1957, and Isard in 1956 [37]. The central idea of industrial location theory deals with the factors consisting of product shipping costs, hence the site for production that is determined by the location factors and companies that are interested to the site with the least location manufacturing costs [35, 36]. Therefore, consideration are taken toward the location accessibility, transportations, and other factors that can affect the operational costs [31].

Although location theory does not explicitly discuss about the regional economic development, its transportation cost modeling is very influential on economic growth and development theory, especially in the field of geography. Prescott and Isard [34] eventually gave a fairly clear picture of regional concepts which are now widely used as Regional Development Science. Analytical methods developed by Borts and Isard [8] and Isard et al. [23] have become a reference standard in conducting regional planning among professionals.

Extensively influenced by the location theory, central place theory broadens the research on the regional development from production field to market field, which brings forward the idea of central place [16]. This theory was built on the assumption that an urban center exists where there are good and services as commodities to be traded [13], hence it became the basis for distribution and spacing in urban and rural areas [18]. Central place theory considers transportation as a crucial aspect for consumers' interest to a product/service [31]. Since the idea of centrality results in the creation of a hierarchy of sites such as cities [26], this theory is significant as the theoretical reference for the study of regional structure [42].

Industry is an effort to produce finished goods, the raw materials of which are obtained through various processing processes at the lowest possible price yet with high quality [40]. The purpose of developing industrial area is to control spatial use, increase efforts in industrial development in the region, increase industrial competitiveness and investment competitiveness, and provide location certainty in terms of infrastructure planning and development in a coordinated manner with related sectors. Regional development for industrial zones also aims to increase investment in the industrial sector. Besides, industrial development can also link local–national development that can further help developing nations transform into developed countries [30, 33].

2.2   Indonesia Masterplan (MP3EI)

The Masterplan for Acceleration and Expansion of Indonesia's Economic Development (abbreviated MP3EI) is a long-term plan created by the Indonesian government in 2011 to accelerate the realization of increasing economic development and to become a developed country by 2025. The creation of MP3EI was to support the national development vision as stipulated in the National Long-Term Development Plan (RPJPN) 2005–2025 and to prepare Indonesia to face various challenges of the globalization era, such as ASEAN Free Trade Area (AFTA).

This masterplan aimed to achieve its vision in creating an independent and prosperous Indonesia, illustrated in the increase of Indonesia's Human Development Index (HDI) that is ready to compete with human resources from other countries. The original plan targeted Indonesia to have per capita income of about USD 14,250–15,500 and gross domestic income (GDP) of about USD 4.0–4.5 trillion, as well as the combination of the real economic growth and the decrease of inflation rate that can reflect the develop country's characteristics.

This vision will be realized through three missions as the main focus, to include (1) increasing added value and expanding the value chain of the production process as well as the distribution of asset management and access of natural resources, geographical areas, and human resources, through the formation of integrated economic activities within and between regions of centers of economic growth; (2) encouraging the actualization of increased production, marketing efficiency, and integration of the domestic market to strengthen the national economy's competitiveness and resilience; (3) encouraging the strengthening of national innovation systems in terms of production, process, and marketing to strengthen sustainable global competitiveness towards innovation-driven economy [2].

To achieve those goals, MP3EI has eight main programs, namely agriculture, mining, energy, industry, maritime, tourism, telematics areas, and the development of strategic areas, which were reduced to 22 main economic activities (see Fig. 1)

There are three elements that must be integrated in the MP3EI implementation strategy, which include (1) development of six economic corridors in Indonesia which was based on the calculation of potential and excellence of each large island, namely Sumatera corridor, Java corridor, Kalimantan corridor, Sulawesi corridor, Bali-Nusa Tenggara corridor, and Maluku-Papua Corridor; (2) improvement of national connectivity that is locally integrated and internationally connected to facilitate the distribution of products and services; and (3) acceleration in the increase of human resource capacity and development of science and technology to support the development of main programs in each economic corridor.

These six corridors have their respective potentials and advantages as the basis for the development of each corridor namely (1) Center for Production and Processing of Natural Products and National Energy Reserves as the theme of Sumatera corridor; (2) National Industry and Service Drivers as the theme of Java corridor; (3) Center for Production and Processing of Mining Products and National Energy Reserves as the theme of Kalimantan corridor; (4) Center for Production and Processing of Agricultural Products, Plantation, Fisheries, Oil and Gas, and National Mining for Sulawesi corridor; (5) Gateway to Tourism and National Food Support as the theme of Bali-Nusa Tenggara

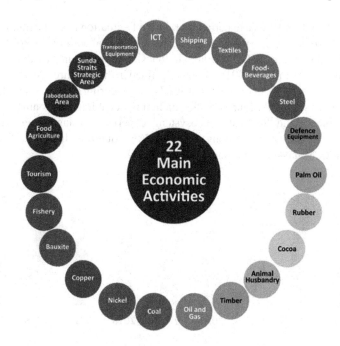

Fig. 1. Main economic activities in MP3EI programs. Source: Bappenas [2]

corridor; and (6) Center for Development of Food, Fisheries, Energy, and National Mining as the theme of Maluku-Papua corridor.

2.3 Economic Development of Indonesia

2.3.1 Achievements

Shifting regional economic developments are often hard to measure, especially in multi-regional contexts. Most statistical estimation involves Gross Domestic Product (GDP) per capita as measurement [1]. However, there are also some measures often used namely Human Development Index that represents the welfare of a region using accountable standardized social data, such as employment, and life expectancy [12], and Global Competitiveness Index (GCI) that captures accurate figure of world economy's potential growth [44].

There are seventeen aspects and three dimensions involved in HDI measure, such as long and healthy life, knowledge, and standard of living to assess the score of each country. Indonesia experienced a stable growth in regards to the score of HDI [41]. In 2015, its HDI score was 0.689 and categorized as medium human development. Currently, the score is 0.707 and marked Indonesia as part of high human development category. Based on this fact, Indonesia sits on 6th spot among ASEAN members behind Singapore (0.935), Brunei (0.845), Malaysia (0.804), Thailand (0.765), and Philippines (0.712). There is an improvement in terms of life expectancy from 69.1 years in 2015 into 71.5 years in 2019, and in terms of GNI/capita from US$ 10,053 to 11,256.

In terms of GCI, Indonesia experienced ranking fluctuation from the initial launched of MP3EI in 2011 until 2019 (see Fig. 2). Indonesia ranked 44th in 2011 and kept decreasing to 50th rank in 2013. Although Indonesian government was able to maintain the spots ranks in 30 s in 2014–2016, another declined in the past three years was occured marking the country 50th out of 141 countries. Despite scoring high in "market size" and "macroeconomic stability", four variables including "enabling environment", "human capital", "markets", and "innovation ecosystem" experience a stagnant growth leading to 0.3 point drop from 2018. Among other ASEAN countries, Indonesia falls behind Singapore (1st), Malaysia (27th) and Thailand (40th).

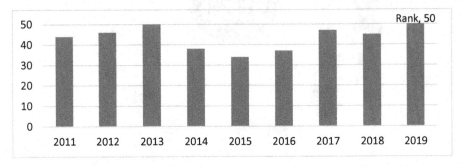

Fig. 2. Indonesia's GCI from 2011–2019. Source: Trading Economics [39]

These figures show that Indonesia is still focusing on variables in efficiency enhancers index related to higher education, labor market efficiency, financial market development, and technological readiness. Indonesia should maximize the supporting factors in order to boost economic development through improvement of some variables including ICT adoption, infrastructure, and labor market. This three variables ranked 72, 72, and 85 out of 141 economies, respectively [43].

Indonesian government has attempted to attract investment in this past decade through foreign and domestic investment. In 2012, investment realization reached US$ 21.6 was from domestic investment [22]. This annual investment realization experienced a steady increase with double digit growth based on year-on-year basis except in 2018 where the growth is only 4.11%. In 2019, the government attract US$ 55.73 billion of investment which FDI and domestic investment almost share similar contribution to investment realization with 52.26% and 47.74% respectively (see Fig. 3). This huge amount of investment expected to gear up economic activities and tackle inequality challenges in various sectors.

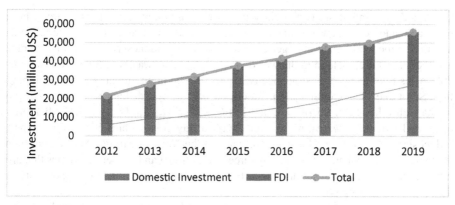

Fig. 3. Indonesia investment realization from 2012–2019. Source: Indonesia Investment Coordinating Board [22]

2.3.2 Potencies

As the fourth most populous country in the world, Indonesia needs to improve its citizens' purchasing power and its goods' objective quality, thus it can be an extraordinary potential for the competitiveness.

It can be seen in Fig. 4 that Indonesia is undergoing a transition in the structure of the productive age, where the decline in the index (ratio) of Indonesian dependence will reach the lowest lift in the period 2020–2030. It shows that the composition of the population of Indonesia with a productive age will reach maximum conditions, which will increase the country's productivity.

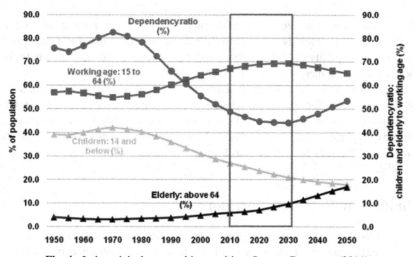

Fig. 4. Indonesia's demographic transition. Source: Bappenas (2011)

In addition, Indonesia is a country that is rich in potential natural resources, both renewable and non-renewable, and is the largest producer of several raw material commodities in the world. In term of geographical potential, Indonesia as a maritime country and the largest archipelago in the world with a total of seawaters of 5.8 million km^2 or 70% of its total territory is strategically located on the main global container shipping line, Sea Lane of Communication. Indonesia has the fourth longest coastline in the world with a length of 95,181 km and has 64 *Large Marine Ecosystem* (LME) territories and 6 direct accesses, namely the Bengala Bay, South China Sea, Sulu Celebes, Indonesian Seas, Arafura-Gulf-Carpentaria, and the North Australian Sea. Indonesia's strategic location because traversed by three international and sea service routes that are effective inter-island transportation facilities. Thus, Indonesia has a huge opportunity to develop its industry globally.

As Indonesia has demographic advantages, abundant natural resources, and strategic location, the masterplan for economic development should be revisited and upgraded in order to improve nation competitiveness as well as people's quality of life.

2.3.3 Challenges

There are some challenges faced by Indonesian government particularly related to inequalities of development among provinces. The government needs to build new economic center outside Java corridor and strengthen logistic network to serve Indonesia as archipelagic country. From economic point of view, the transportation network connected to the center of production and nodes of consumption will generate volume of movement accompanied by a decrease cost of distribution, leading to the improvement of national economy. For this reason, strengthening inter-and intra-island connectivities need to take into account the distribution of specific economic growth nodes along with linkages between surrounding regions in order to create inter-regional economic equality.

Indonesia needs to utilize digital infrastructure to encourage regional development since information technology plays a crucial role in increasing innovation and productivity, improving quality of life, competitiveness and economic modernization, bridging economic and social inequality, and alleviating poverty in the long run.

However, Indonesia needs a huge amount of investment cost to develop all the sectors. Therefore, searching for alternative schemes for economic development is mandatory. Despite having numerous funding schemes, such as state budget, private equity, and public private partnership, both central and local government have not utilized those schemes due to various reasons such as limited knowledge, complex adminstration and many others.

3 Indonesian Economic Corridors

Indonesia has been regarded as one of successful nations in transforming its economic growth since the country independence in 1945. Indonesia's economy experienced a stable growth and only contracted twice since 1961. Its highest GDP growth was recorded in 1968 or in the beginning of the New Order era reaching 10.92%. While in the Reformation era, the highest economic growth was recorded in 2007 with 6.35%. Indonesia's economy experienced a negative growth during the Old Order era in 1963 and during the Asian financial crisis that was accompanied by riots throughout the country with a deep contraction of -13.13% in 1998 [10].

Economic growth of a country is expected to improve people's quality of life and living standards through an adequate income for all households. However, there is a growing concern regarding imbalance income between urban and rural households and a gap of economic distribution between the western and eastern part of Indonesia in the past fifty years. This issue of income disparities have contributed to the increasing cost of transportation between western and eastern region and limited competitiveness from the eastern part to contribute for the overall gross domestic product of the country. The strategy of economic corridor is argued as one of the solution to accelerate and to expand economic development in equal manner.

Indonesian regimes had initiated grand design of economic development in order to improve nation's competitiveness by taking into account different approaches and focusses since country's independence. For instance, Old Order era introduced Kasimo Plan to improve economic activities by focusing on self-sufficiency in agriculture sector. On the other hand, New order era started to organize economic activities and divide them into several priorities documented through Five-year Development Plan or *Rencana Pembangunan Lima Tahun* (REPELITA). In addition, the government issued a Master Plan for the Acceleration and Expansion of Indonesia's Economic Development (MP3EI) for national economic grand design to cope with various issues related to poverty, economic disparities, and global challenges in 2010.

The objectives of MP3EI to increase benefit and to expand the value chain of the production process and distribution of asset management and access of natural resources, geographical areas, and human resources can be obtained through the creation of integrated and synergic economic activities between economic centers. In general the masterplan divided economic activities based on potential and advantages of each region across Indonesia. It divided into six corridors consist of Sumatera, Java, Kalimantan, Sulawesi, Bali-Nusa Tenggara, and Maluku-Papua where each corridor has different focus of development. Sumatera serve as center of agricultural products and national energy reserves, Java as center of industry and services, Kalimantan as plantation and mining center. While Bali-Nusa Tenggara serves as tourism and food support, Sulawesi as center of agriculture and fishery, and Maluku-Papua as energy and mining center.

3.1 Sumatera Corridor

Sumatera as the center for production and processing of natural resources and energy reserves strategically located in economic trading activities from Europe, Africa, South Asia, East Asia and Australia. Despite its potential location, the economic condition of Sumatera exposes a huge gap between provinces and urban-rural disparities regarding economic, health, and education. Average income of this corridor is supported from natural resources industries such as palm oil, rubber, and coal. Other potential sector such as shipping have been also prioritized by the government to support steel industrial development in the southern part of the island.

Overall, gross domestic regional product (GRDP) per capita from ten provinces in Sumatera corridor experience a stable growth in the past five years during 2014–2018 period (see Table 1). The average GRDP per capita for all provinces was ranging from US$ 1,450 to US$ 5,470. Most provinces with high GRDP per capita have potential industries in natural resources (Riau and Riau Achipelago) or act as business center such as South Sumatera and North Sumatera. On the other hand, the result from GRDP per capita was not linear to the GDP shares. For instance, Riau Achipelago and Jambi with competitive GRDP per capita evidently showed to have limited contribution to the national economic growth by 1.69% and 1.36% respectively, leaving Riau and North Sumatera as two highest ranking in term of GDP contribution.

3.2 Java Corridor

Java corridor is argued as the driver for national industry and service provision. This corridor is the most populous islands and has contributed as the highest economic activities among other regions. This corridor transforms raw materials into tertiary industries similar to those located in Singapore, Shenzhen, and Dubai. The main focus of Java corridor is food and beverage industry, textiles, and vehicle equipment. There are other potential industries such as shipping, ICT, and defense equipment.

Overall, GRDP per capita from six provinces in Java corridor experienced a huge gap between DKI Jakarta as the capital city with remaining provinces (see Table 2). GRDP per capita of DKI Jakarta reaches US$ 10,380 while the rest provinces were ranging from US$ US$ 1,630 to US$ 2,490. This high differences raised inequalities issue such as high differences income, growth disparity throughout the value chain, lack of domestic and foreign investment and insufficient infrastructure to accomodate larger economic activities. Despite disparities in GRDP per capita between provinces in Java corridor, share of GRDP from these provinces were ranked as the highest one to national economic growth. Three provinces that play a significant role as the main contributor are DKI Jakarta (17.05%), East Java (14.58%), and West Java (13.05%) respectively.

3.3 Kalimantan Corridor

The development of Kalimantan economic corridor is focused on national energy reserves where the island has a large number of oil and gas reserves, coal, and other minerals compared to other corridors in the country. In addition, there are other potential industries that can be expanded for economic growth such as palm oil, wood, steel and bauxite industries. This potential materials are concentrated in a little number of locations including Pontianak, Palangkaraya, Banjarmasin, and Samarinda.

GRDP per capita from five provinces in Kalimantan corridor shows different figure where two provinces, East Kalimantan and North Kalimantan had a high GRDP per capita compared to the rest of provinces in the corridor (see Table 3). GRDP per capita of West Kalimantan, Central Kalimantan, and South Kalimantan remained low ranging from US$ 1,680 to US$ 2,270. GDP shares showed disparities of contribution in this corridor where only one province of East Kalimantan that highly contributed to national economic growth.

Table 1. GRDP per capita and distribution per province in Sumatera corridor (2014–2018)

Provinces	2014	2015	2016	2017	2018	2014–2018
GRDP per capita (Thousand US$)*						
Aceh	1.60	1.55	1.57	1.61	1.66	1.60
North Sumatera	2.10	2.18	2.27	2.36	2.45	2.27
West Sumatera	1.79	1.87	1.94	2.02	2.10	1.94
Riau	4.99	4.88	4.87	4.88	4.88	4.90
Jambi	2.47	2.53	2.60	2.68	2.76	2.61
South Sumatera	2.11	2.18	2.26	2.35	2.46	2.27
Bengkulu	1.35	1.40	1.45	1.50	1.55	1.45
Lampung	1.63	1.70	1.76	1.84	1.91	1.77
Bangka Belitung	2.27	2.31	2.35	2.41	2.47	2.36
Riau Archipelago	5.26	5.42	5.54	5.50	5.61	5.47
GRDP distribution to GDP (%)						
Aceh	1.2	1.11	1.08	1.06	1.04	1.10
North Sumatera	4.89	4.91	4.96	4.98	4.95	4.94
West Sumatera	1.54	1.54	1.55	1.56	1.54	1.55
Riau	6.36	5.6	5.4	5.13	5.04	5.51
Jambi	1.36	1.33	1.36	1.38	1.39	1.36
South Sumatera	2.87	2.85	2.8	2.79	2.8	2.82
Bengkulu	0.42	0.43	0.44	0.44	0.44	0.43
Lampung	2.16	2.17	2.21	2.23	2.23	2.20
Bangka Belitung	0.53	0.52	0.52	0.51	0.49	0.51
Riau Archipelago	1.69	1.71	1.71	1.66	1.66	1.69

*In Constant Price (2010)

3.4 Sulawesi Corridor

This corridor is focused on agricultural production and processing such as cocoa plantations, fisheries, and oil and gas and mining particularly related to nickel production. This

Table 2. GRDP per capita and distribution per province in Java corridor (2014–2018)

Provinces	2014	2015	2016	2017	2018	2014–2018
GRDP per capita (Thousand US$)*						
DKI Jakarta	9.40	9.86	10.33	10.87	11.44	10.38
West Java	1.72	1.78	1.86	1.93	2.01	1.86
Central Java	1.57	1.65	1.72	1.80	1.88	1.72
DIY	1.51	1.56	1.63	1.69	1.78	1.63
East Java	2.26	2.36	2.48	2.60	2.73	2.49
Banten	2.06	2.13	2.19	2.27	2.36	2.20
GRDP distribution to GDP (%)						
DKI Jakarta	16.5	17.07	17.11	17.21	17.34	17.05
West Java	12.97	13.09	13.1	13.01	13.09	13.05
Central Java	8.64	8.68	8.61	8.53	8.47	8.59
DIY	0.87	0.87	0.87	0.87	0.87	0.87
East Java	14.4	14.52	14.7	14.65	14.61	14.58
Banten	4.01	4.11	4.1	4.1	4.1	4.08

*In Constant Price (2010)

corridor is planned as a market provider for East Asia, Australia, Ocenia, and America. However, there are several challenges faced by this corridor including low GRDP compared with other corridors, low attractiveness of investment, and inadequate supporting infrastructure such as roads, electricity, water, and health across provinces. Although this corridor experienced of gradual economic growth in the past years and recorded as the highest economic growth of 6.65% in 2019 [9], the contribution of Sulawesi to GDP remained low. This corridor ranked fourth after Java, Sumatera, and Kalimantan respectively.

In term of GRDP per capita in Sulawesi corridor, the result showed a little gap among six provinces between US$ 1,410 to US$ 2,170 (see Table 4). Similar with Kalimantan corridor, contributor to the GDP was mainly from South Sulawesi province with 2.96%. While other provinces only have limited contribution less than 1% similar with Bengkulu and Bangka Belitung in Sumatera corridor, DIY in Java corridor, and Central Kalimantan and North Kalimantan in Kalimantan corridor.

3.5 Bali-Nusa Tenggara Corridor

Bali is well-known as for its natural beauty with the volcanic mountains, beaches, and cultural preservation. Thus this corridor is focused on tourism and national food support that is expected to improve the people's economic stability, which 17% of them experience income disparities between Bali and Nusa Tenggara. Report from Statistics Indonesia showed three main activities to increase regional economic growth considering their annual increase of 11% including livestock, fisheries, and tourism.

Table 3. GRDP per capita and distribution per province in Kalimantan corridor (2014–2018)

Provinces	2014	2015	2016	2017	2018	2014–2018
GRDP per capita (Thousand US$)*						
West Kalimantan	1.57	1.62	1.68	1.74	1.80	1.68
Central Kalimantan	2.08	2.18	2.27	2.37	2.45	2.27
South Kalimantan	1.88	1.92	1.97	2.04	2.11	1.98
East Kalimantan	9.18	8.87	8.65	8.73	8.79	8.84
North Kalimantan	5.32	5.30	5.29	5.44	5.57	5.38
GRDP distribution to GDP (%)						
West Kalimantan	1.24	1.26	1.28	1.29	1.29	1.27
Central Kalimantan	0.84	0.86	0.89	0.92	0.93	0.89
South Kalimantan	1.2	1.18	1.16	1.16	1.15	1.17
East Kalimantan	4.94	4.33	4.03	4.31	4.26	4.37
North Kalimantan	0.55	0.53	0.52	0.56	0.57	0.55

*In Constant Price (2010)

In term of GRDP per capita in this corridor, the result showed a gap among the three provinces (see Table 5). Bali has income two times higher than NTB and almost three times higher than NTT due to high traffic from domestic and international tourists each year. Despite the high volume tourism sector in Bali, the contribution to national GDP remained insignificant compared with other provinces. Bali only contributed 1.52% to national economic growth, while the two provinces below 1%.

3.6 Maluku-Papua Corridor

Maluku and Papua corridor is expected as the center for food, fisheries, energy and national mining. This is supported by several economic activities in seven economic centers such as Sofifi and Ambon in Maluku region and Sorong, Manokwari, Timika, Jayapura and Merauku in Papua island. This province has abundant natural resource potential particularly in mining sector. This sector has contributed more than 50% of the Papuan economy, with copper, gold, oil, and gas are highly ranked in term of economic activities across the province.

Table 4. GRDP per capita and distribution per province in Sulawesi corridor (2014–2018)

Provinces	2014	2015	2016	2017	2018	2014–2018
GRDP per capita (Thousand US$)*						
North Sulawesi	1.92	2.01	2.12	2.23	2.34	2.12
Central Sulawesi	1.75	1.98	2.15	2.27	2.37	2.10
South Sulawesi	1.91	2.03	2.16	2.29	2.43	2.17
Southeast Sulawesi	1.92	2.01	2.10	2.20	2.30	2.11
Gorontalo	1.28	1.34	1.41	1.48	1.55	1.41
West Sulawesi	1.33	1.40	1.45	1.52	1.59	1.46
GRDP distribution to GDP (%)						
North Sulawesi	0.76	0.78	0.8	0.8	0.8	0.79
Central Sulawesi	0.84	0.92	0.95	0.97	1.01	0.94
South Sulawesi	2.79	2.92	2.99	3.03	3.09	2.96
Southeast Sulawesi	0.74	0.75	0.77	0.78	0.79	0.77
Gorontalo	0.24	0.24	0.25	0.25	0.25	0.25
West Sulawesi	0.28	0.28	0.28	0.29	0.29	0.28

*In Constant Price (2010)

Despite its potential resources, the economic condition of Papua still exposes a huge gap not only inside the corridor but also compared with other islands in western part of the country regarding economic, health, and education. This can be seen from the contribution of GRDP of the corridor that was less than 2% from the four provinces. The GRDP per capita between Maluku and Papua has significant gap (see Table 6). Papua and West Papua are the two provinces act as the center of mining sector, therefore it is common they relatively earned rather adequate income than their neighbouring provinces that depend on daily activities in fisheries or other sectors. This corridor also faces major obstacles that limit their economic growth including high risk and uncertainty due to high intensity of riots, low population with low level of productivity, and limited supporting infrastructure.

Table 5. GRDP per capita and distribution per province in Bali-Nusa Tenggara corridor (2014–2018)

Provinces	2014	2015	2016	2017	2018	2014–2018
GRDP per capita (Thousand US$)*						
Bali	2.05	2.14	2.25	2.35	2.48	2.26
NTB	1.06	1.27	1.33	1.32	1.24	1.25
NTT	0.74	0.76	0.79	0.82	0.85	0.79
GRDP distribution to GDP (%)						
Bali	1.46	1.51	1.54	1.55	1.56	1.52
NTB	0.76	0.91	0.92	0.9	0.83	0.86
NTT	0.64	0.65	0.66	0.66	0.66	0.65

*In Constant Price (2010)

Table 6. GRDP per capita and distribution per province in Maluku-Papua corridor (2014–2018)

Provinces	2014	2015	2016	2017	2018	2014–2018
GRDP per capita (Thousand US$)*						
Maluku	0.98	1.02	1.06	1.10	1.15	1.06
North Maluku	1.16	1.21	1.25	1.32	1.40	1.27
West Papua	4.08	4.14	4.22	4.29	4.45	4.24
Papua	2.71	2.85	3.06	3.14	3.32	3.02
GRDP distribution to GDP (%)						
Maluku	0.3	0.29	0.29	0.29	0.29	0.29
North Maluku	0.23	0.23	0.23	0.23	0.24	0.23
West Papua	0.54	0.54	0.53	0.52	0.53	0.53
Papua	1.25	1.29	1.37	1.37	1.41	1.34

*In Constant Price (2010)

4   Methodology and Data Sources

This study uses the qualitative study to generate the research objectives by combining desk study, benchmarking and series of an in-depth interview [5]. Desk study initiated by extracting previous reports from government institutions and other supporting documents related to MP3EI. This is a crucial step to produce a baseline for further evaluation and generate targeted output [7, 21].

Following the desk study, other project or documents from neighboring and developed countries which may experience similar situation were evaluated through benchmarking process, which is argued as a way to measure indicators and to compare one case to another that leads data sharing from best practice to the investigated context in the research [24, 46]. The benchmarking process is expected to find the gap between Indonesia and other countries in developing a national economic plan through industrial clusters.

A series of in-depth interviews with government officials was conducted to obtain primary sources of existing problems and suggestions. There are numerous methods to generate stakeholders' perspective such as questionnaire surveys, dialogues, workshop and focus group discussion [25, 45]. However, since these approaches require commitment and time flexibility for government officials due to their packed daily activities in the ministries, therefore in-depth interview held in their location and matched their time availability is the best way in extracting information [28].

The in-depth interviews were conducted with five individuals from the public agencies including the Ministry of Transportation, Ministry of Public Works, National Planning Agency, and Ministry of Finance, and Ministry of Industry and Trade. With such respondents, their inputs are considered crucial for research evaluation and validation. The interviews were lasted for about 15 min to 30 min depending on the respondent's availability to collect sufficient data for analysis. There were two surveyors taking notes because most of the respondents were unwilling to be audiotaped during interview. Surveyors' notes were crosschecked to reduce misinterpretation and increase the validity of the data.

5 Indonesia Masterplan Revisited

5.1 Sumatera Corridor

Based on the analysis from Berawi et al. (2017), potential industries in Sumatera Corridor are focused on plantation crops which may consist of coconut, palm, rubber, sugar cane, coffee, pepper. With ten provinces located in Sumatera island, each province will have different attributes of industry, some of them may not have allocated. There are two types of development, plantation system and processing industry. Each location will have different industry depends on the availability of resources, human resources capability, supporting infrastructure and local regulation. In general, there are eleven processing industries spread across provinces for ten plantation types. Most industries have two locations for the processing industry except for coconut that has three locations in North Sumatera, Riau, and Jambi, and pepper that has only one location in Bangka Belitung.

Coconut processing industry will be constructed in Riau and Jambi provinces since Riau has potential area of palm plantations about 440,821 ha. The province also has a port near Indragiri Hilir – one of the largest palm plantation (85% from palm plantations in the province) in Riau namely Guntung Harbor. On the other hand, the largest coconut commodity in Jambi is located in Tanjung Jabung Timur regency. The regency supported by Muara Sabak Port contributes 58,676 ha or around 49% of the total area of Jambi coconut plantations. The detail of industrial development in Sumatera corridor can be seen in Fig. 5.

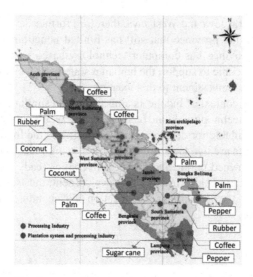

Fig. 5. Potential industries in Sumatera corridor

As infrastructure is highly correlated with regional development [32], Indonesian government has initiated Trans-Sumatera Toll Road development to facilitate the mobility of economic activities and industrial areas in Sumatera corridor. Despite its positive impact for the region's economic growth, this 2,788 km road network system that connects the northern part to southern part of Sumatera is still only feasible in a few selected parts of the network. To increase the project feasibility, a research done by Berawi et al. [6] has attempted to create an alternative concept for this project by coming up with a new route that took into account the GDRP and population density in its selection method. That research produced an optimum route for the Northern part of Sumatera that comprises Nanggroe Aceh Darusalam province with its processing industry in Lhoksumawe as well as mining industry in Aceh Utara dan Aceh Timur, and North Sumatera province with its processing industry in Batubara and agriculture and mining industry in Langkat.

5.2 Java Corridor

Java corridor will be developed as information and communication technology (ICT) industry both hardware and software. Hardware is required to support computing system and this hardware industry will consist of an integrated semiconductor factory, and gadget assembly factory. Meanwhile, the software industry will consist of game development, mobile application, and animation accommodated in one area called technopark.

The locations of the semiconductor industry will be in three provinces Banten, West Java, and Central Java. Banten and West Java Provinces have great potential in terms of metal goods industry, computers, electronic goods, optics and electrical equipment. Therefore, development of semiconductor industry in those provinces will excel in existing industries for export and domestic consumption. Meanwhile, Central Java is selected as one of the locations of the semiconductor industry due to abundant raw materials of silicon. Furthermore, since gadget assembly plants can be commonly found in DKI

Jakarta, Banten, Central Java and West Java, therefore further development in this area should be focused in the province that still has limited penetration of this plant such as East Java. This province has computer technology-based universities, namely the Surabaya State Polytechnic to support the human resources as well as competitive labor costs which may attract investment to this location.

Technopark in the context of Indonesia aims to adopt a similar concept in San Francisco, California. The technopark should be supported by well-educated human resources and adequate land available for development. According to the Indonesia's HDI score, Jakarta and Yogyakarta are two locations that provide a high HDI score. Both locations are supported by renowned public and private universities ready for occupation. Land availability in Yogyakarta is also feasible for development, thus selecting this province as technopark is one of the best options. The location of each industry in the Java corridor can be seen in Fig. 6.

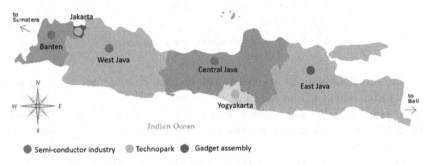

Fig. 6. Potential industries in Java corridor

As need for infrastructure development for facilitating the regional economic activities has increased throughout the country as well as in Java island, Indonesian government has planned to develop several new railway networks, including high speed railway that connects Jakarta and Bandung city. This project that will stretch at about 142 km between Halim, Karawang, Walini and Tegalluar stations is expected to improve connectivity for both cities to further encourage new urban development.

A study conducted by Berawi et al. [3] attempted to develop Walini, an area that will be connected to the Jakarta-Bandung high-speed rail line, as a new IT-based city and technopark by adding value to increase its competitiveness regarding infrastructure, technological readiness, and urban development.

Developed as an IT-based city concept, high-tech industry is allocated space inside New Walini city in the conceptual planning, with six areas of development from residential, commercial, and offices, to high-tech industry, research universities, and open space. The allocation for buildings is 55.95% while the rest is for open space area. The buildings consist of 36.88% for residential, 5.53% for offices, 8.85% for commercial, 4.69% for high-tech industry, and 9% for research university.

Furthermore, to support its activities as techno park, an area for research and development (R&D) is allocated in the eastern part of the city, in which it will be supported by offices, high-tech industries, a research university, and residential building. The zoning locates all R&D area in one location to accommodate the mobility of the research output from academic-based researchers into practice in professional realm (see Fig. 7).

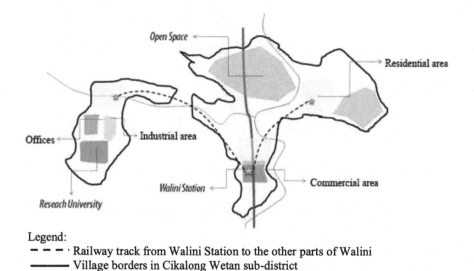

Legend:
− − − · Railway track from Walini Station to the other parts of Walini
───── Village borders in Cikalong Wetan sub-district

Fig. 7. New Walini city development map. Source: Berawi et al [4]

5.3 Kalimantan Corridor

Kalimantan Corridor encountered a problem related to the quality of coal resources and a negative impact on the environment based on the current mining system. In order to improve such problems, coal smelter is proposed to build in Kalimantan located in East Kalimantan and South Kalimantan provinces. The locations selected based on their sufficient resources from raw material, labor, and transportation such as roads and ports. Both also contribute to national GDP in terms of coal production by 236,613,732.47 tons and 148,845,555.32 tons respectively. The detail of industrial development in Kalimantan corridor can be seen as Fig. 8.

5.4 Sulawesi Corridor

Potential industry in Sulawesi Corridor is related to fishery including aquaculture, fresh-water resources and processing. Their development can be divided into two types based on the system and storage as well as processing industry. For aquaculture, there are several commodities such as snapper, grouper, giant trevally and seaweed. The potential of aquaculture located in North Sulawesi, Southeast Sulawesi, and South Sulawesi. In each province, a Smart Floating Farms and cold storage will be built to store aquaculture and capture fisheries. Both types of manufacturing are required close to the coastal area and the catch fishery dock to integrate storage and catch monitoring.

Fig. 8. Potential industries in Kalimantan corridor

Snapper exists in North Sulawesi, South Sulawesi, and Southeast Sulawesi. The average capture of red and white snapper in the three provinces reaches 500–3,000 tons per year. From this figure, it indicates that the fish processing capacity of 20–30 tons per day is sufficient for all fish captures. Therefore, each province requires one integrated snapper processing plants. On the other hand, seaweed commodities will located in the two largest potential seaweed areas, namely Takalar and Bantaeng of South Sulawesi, and in the processing factory in Palu, Central Sulawesi due to their closeness to the sea and seaweed area. South Sulawesi is also proposed for chitin and chitosan processing through a biochemistry industry that will be located in Pinrang and Barru, as well as milkfish processing plant located in Bajo regency. The composition of industrial development in Sulawesi corridor can be seen in Fig. 9.

5.5 Bali-Nusa Tenggara Corridor

This corridor will be developed based on the tourism sector due to the high potential of its natural resources and existing tourism attracted both domestic and foreign tourists. Some of its infrastructure should be improved in order to increase the value of tourism in this corridor. For instance, Bali province requires transportation improvement as the ownership of private vehicles has exponentially increased which leads to traffic jam that may reduce tourist comfort in the future. One potential transportation development is the tram system due to forbidden elevated construction and high cost for the underground. Moreover, Nusa Tenggara that comprises Nusa Tenggara Barat and Nusa Tenggara Timur requires port construction and access to electricity. The former for the better accessibility among islands and the latter to increase services for local people and tourists.

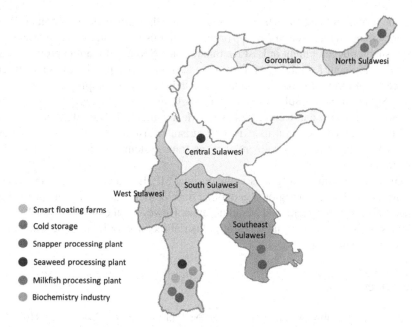

Fig. 9. Potential industries in Sulawesi corridor

5.6 Papua-Maluku Corridor

This corridor has commodities in mining such as copper and gold metal. However, Papua area is the only exploited one compared to Maluku archipelago. Buru island in Maluku has mining resources but it is still currently executed in the traditional way by local people. Some of them also use dangerous methods and materials, thus smelter development for mining processing is a required in Papua and Maluku provinces.

6   Conclusion

Industrial development plays a significant role in increasing national economic growth and improving the competitiveness of a nation on a global scale. Low economic growth experienced by Indonesia may come as the result of limited industrial expansion and the failure to map the potential development in the previous initiatives properly. The industry sectors rank as the top contributors to Indonesia's economic growth, thus the existing industrial clusters should be evaluated to accelerate greater economic expansion. This research categorizes industrial development based on the previous report, which divided into six economic corridors from Sumatra, Java, Kalimantan, Sulawesi, Bali-Nusa Tenggara, and Papua-Maluku.

The research generates the focus of industrial development for each corridor. Sumatera will be focused on the development of plantation processing industry with the support of infrastructure development planned by government such as Trans-Sumatera Toll Road, while ICT industry will be located in Java corridor by proposing new IT-based city such as the one in Walini that has been conceptually studied. Kalimantan and Maluku-Papua corridors will be encouraged to develop processing industry of natural resources, including coal smelter development in East Kalimantan and South Kalimantan provinces, and smelter development for mining processing in Maluku-Papua provinces. Sulawesi corridor need to improve its existing aquaculture industry by developing fish processing in North Sulawesi, South Sulawesi, and Southeast Sulawesi, seaweed-processing factories in South Sulawesi dan Central Sulawesi. Meanwhile, Bali-Nusa Tenggara corridor should be developed based on its existing tourism industry with the support of transportation infrastructure improvement such as tram system in Bali and port in Nusa Tenggara.

Some of development programs in the original MP3EI masterplan is still reliable to face current challenges to regional economic development such as in Sumatera, Kalimantan, Bali-Nusa Tenggara, and Maluku-Papua. However, other corridors such as Java and Sulawesi need to switch the focus of industrial sector in order to cope with current practice and arising challenges.

References

1. Aitken, A.: Measuring welfare beyond GDP. Natl. Inst. Econ. Rev. **249**(1), R3–R16 (2019). https://doi.org/10.1177/002795011924900110
2. Bappenas: Master Plan Percepatan dan Perluasan Pembangunan Ekonomi Indonesia (MP3EI) 2011–2025. http://www.bappenas.go.id/id/berita-dan-siaran-pers/perkembangan-ekonomi-indonesia-dan-dunia-triwulan-ii-tahun-2019/. https://www.bappenas.go.id/id/berita-dan-sia ran-pers/narasi-tunggal-indonesia-development-forum-memerangi-ketimpangan-untuk-per tumbuhan-yang-lebih-baik/. Accessed 05 June 2020
3. Berawi, M.A., et al.: Analysis of life cycle cost and public-private partnership in the development of Walini City as technology park. Int. J. Technol. **9**(7), 1469–1479 (2018). https://doi.org/10.14716/ijtech.v9i7.2588
4. Berawi, M.A., et al.: Increasing added value for the New City of Walini through infrastructure project development. Int. J. Technol. **8**(6), 1141–1149 (2017). https://doi.org/10.14716/ijtech.v8i6.755
5. Berawi, M.A., et al.: Prioritizing airport development plan to optimize financial feasibility. Aviation **22**(3), 115–128 (2018). https://doi.org/10.3846/aviation.2018.6589
6. Berawi, M.A., et al.: Producing alternative concept for the trans-sumatera toll road project development using location quotient method. Procedia Eng. 265–273 (2017). https://doi.org/10.1016/j.proeng.2017.01.334
7. von Blottnitz, H., Curran, M.A.: A review of assessments conducted on bio-ethanol as a transportation fuel from a net energy, greenhouse gas, and environmental life cycle perspective. J. Clean. Prod. **15**(7), 607–619 (2007). https://doi.org/10.1016/j.jclepro.2006.03.002
8. Borts, G.H., Isard, W.: Methods of regional analysis: an introduction to regional science. Economica **29**(113), 97 (1962)
9. BPS-Statistics Indonesia: Pertumbuhan Ekonomi dan Kontribusi terhadap PDB Nasional per Pulau (2019). https://databoks.katadata.co.id/datapublish/2020/02/06/sulawesi-pulau-dengan-pertumbuhan-ekonomi-terbesar-2019
10. BPS-Statistics Indonesia: Pertumbuhan Ekonomi Indonesia (1961–2018). https://databoks.katadata.co.id/datapublish/2018/01/31/inilah-pertumbuhan-ekonomi-indonesia-sejak-1961. Accessed 29 May 2020

11. Cameron, G.C., Hoover, E.M.: An introduction to regional economics. Econ. J. **82**(328), 1447 (1972). https://doi.org/10.2307/2231342
12. Cameron, M.: J. Dev. Persp. Dept. of Economics, Adekunle Ajasin University (2005)
13. Capello, R.: Regional growth and local development theories: conceptual evolution over fifty years of regional science. Geogr. Econ. Soc. **11**(1), 9–21 (2009). https://doi.org/10.3166/ges. 11.9-21
14. Capello, R., Nijkamp, P.: Regional growth and development theories revisited. In: Endogenous Regional Development: Perspectives, Measurement and Empirical Investigation, pp. 301–324 (2011). https://doi.org/10.4337/9781849804783.00020
15. Carree, M.A., Thurik, A.R.: The impact of entrepreneurship on economic growth. In: Handbook of Entrepreneurship Research, pp. 557–594 (2010). https://doi.org/10.1007/978-1-4419-1191-9_20
16. Dauphiné, A.: Theories of geographical locations. In: Geographical Models with Mathematica, pp. 115–128 (2017). https://doi.org/10.1016/b978-1-78548-225-0.50006-3
17. Dawkins, C.J.: Regional development theory: conceptual foundations, classic works, and recent developments. J. Plan. Lit. **18**(2), 131–171 (2003). https://doi.org/10.1177/088541220 3254706
18. Demarco, M., Matusitz, J.: The impact of central-place theory on Wal-Mart. J. Hum. Behav. Soc. Environ. **21**(2), 130–141 (2011). https://doi.org/10.1080/10911359.2011.542991
19. Démurger, S.: Infrastructure development and economic growth: an explanation for regional disparities in China? J. Comp. Econ. **29**(1), 95–117 (2001). https://doi.org/10.1006/jcec.2000. 1693
20. Fingleton, B., Fischer, M.M.: Neoclassical theory versus new economic geography: competing explanations of cross-regional variation in economic development. Ann. Reg. Sci. **44**(3), 467–491 (2010). https://doi.org/10.1007/s00168-008-0278-z
21. Henry, R.K., et al.: Municipal solid waste management challenges in developing countries - Kenyan case study. Waste Manage. **26**(1), 92–100 (2006). https://doi.org/10.1016/j.wasman. 2005.03.007
22. Indonesia Investment Coordinating Board: Investment Realization. https://www.bkpm.go.id/ id/statistik/investasi-langsung-luar-negeri-fdi. Accessed 01 June 2020
23. Isard, W., et al.: Gravity and spatial interaction models. In: Methods of Interregional and Regional Analysis, pp. 243–280 (2018). https://doi.org/10.4324/9781315249056-6
24. Išoraite, M.: Benchmarking methodology in a transport sector. Transport **19**(6), 269–275 (2004). https://doi.org/10.1080/16484142.2004.9637986
25. Jepsen, A.L., Eskerod, P.: Stakeholder analysis in projects: challenges in using current guidelines in the real world. Int. J. Proj. Manage. **27**(4), 335–343 (2009). https://doi.org/10.1016/ j.ijproman.2008.04.002
26. Knitter, D., et al.: Integrated centrality analysis: a diachronic comparison of selected Western Anatolian locations. Quat. Int. **312**, 45–56 (2013). https://doi.org/10.1016/j.quaint.2013. 04.020
27. Kuhlman, J.M., et al.: The economics of location. Land Econ. **31**(2), 162 (1955). https://doi. org/10.2307/3159631
28. Liu, H.C., et al.: Induced aggregation operators in the VIKOR method and its application in material selection. Appl. Math. Model. **37**(9), 6325–6338 (2013). https://doi.org/10.1016/j. apm.2013.01.026
29. Marks, G., Hooghe, L.: Optimality and authority: a critique of neoclassical theory. J. Common Mark. Stud. **38**(5), 795–816 (2000). https://doi.org/10.1111/1468-5965.00265
30. Monastiriotis, V.: Regional growth and national development: transition in Central and Eastern Europe and the regional Kuznets curve in the East and the West. Spat. Econ. Anal. **9**(2), 142–161 (2014). https://doi.org/10.1080/17421772.2014.891156

31. Mosler, K.: Mathematical location and land use theory: an introduction. Locat. Sci. **5**(3), 205–206 (1997). https://doi.org/10.1016/s0966-8349(98)00000-x
32. Nijkamp, P.: Spatial dynamics, innovation and infrastructure: a long wave view of regional development in developing and developed countries. In: Chatterji, M. (ed.) Technology Transfer in the Developing Countries, pp. 76–93. Palgrave Macmillan, London (1990). https://doi.org/10.1007/978-1-349-20558-5_6
33. Pike, A., et al.: Shifting horizons in local and regional development. Reg. Stud. **51**(1), 46–57 (2017). https://doi.org/10.1080/00343404.2016.1158802
34. Prescott, J.R., Isard, W.: Introduction to Regional Science. J. Am. Stat. Assoc. **71**(353), 243 (1976). https://doi.org/10.2307/2285779
35. Qu, J., Ma, C.: Regional development theory and its instructions for regional culture industry development. Presented at the (2013). https://doi.org/10.1109/nces.2012.6543585
36. Snieska, V., et al.: Evaluation of location's attractiveness for business growth in smart development. Econ. Res. Istraz. **32**(1), 925–946 (2019). https://doi.org/10.1080/1331677X.2019.1590217
37. Stimson, R.J., et al.: Regional economic development: analysis and planning strategy. (2006). https://doi.org/10.1007/3-540-34829-8
38. Timmer, M.P., et al.: Economic growth in Europe: a comparative industry perspective. (2010). https://doi.org/10.1017/CBO9780511762703
39. Trading Economics: Indonesia Competitiveness Rank | 2007–2019 Data | 2020–2022 Forecast | Historical. https://tradingeconomics.com/indonesia/competitiveness-rank. Accessed 01 June 2020
40. United Nations Conference on Trade and Development: Technology and Innovation Report 2015, Geneva (2015)
41. United Nations Development Programme: Human Development Reports. http://hdr.undp.org/en/countries/profiles/IDN. Accessed 01 June 2020
42. Vionis, A.K., Papantoniou, G.: Central place theory reloaded and revised: political economy and landscape dynamics in the longue Durée (2019). https://doi.org/10.3390/land8020036
43. World Economic Forum: Global Competitiveness Report 2019. http://www3.weforum.org/docs/WEF_TheGlobalCompetitivenessReport2019.pdf. Accessed 01 June 2020
44. Xia, R., et al.: Is global competitive index a good standard to measure economic growth? A suggestion for improvement. Int. J. Serv. Stand. **8**(1), 45–57 (2012). https://doi.org/10.1504/IJSS.2012.048438
45. Yang, F., et al.: Urban design to lower summertime outdoor temperatures: an empirical study on high-rise housing in Shanghai. Build. Environ. **46**(3), 769–785 (2011). https://doi.org/10.1016/j.buildenv.2010.10.010
46. Zulkarnain, Z., et al.: Developing an intelligent logistics and distribution system for a large number of retail outlets: a big data analytics approach. CSID J. Infrastruct. Dev. **3**(1), 28 (2020). https://doi.org/10.32783/csid-jid.v3i1.106

Blue Economy as a Policy-Driven Innovation System: Research Funding and the Direction of Ocean-Related Innovation

Cristina Sousa[1,2](✉) (iD), Margarida Fontes[3] (iD), and Oscarina Conceição[1,4] (iD)

[1] Iscte - Instituto Universitário de Lisboa, DINÂMIA'CET, Lisbon, Portugal
`cristina.sousa@iscte-iul.pt, oconceicao@ipca.pt`
[2] Univ Portucalense, Research on Economics, Management and Information Technologies
– REMIT, Porto, Portugal
[3] LNEG – National Laboratory of Energy and Geology, Lisbon, Portugal
`margarida.fontes@lneg.pt`
[4] Polytechnic Institute of Cávado and Ave, Barcelos, Portugal

Abstract. The "Blue Economy" has been identified as a driver of European growth, through the development of new competences and activities that enable a sustainable exploitation of ocean resources. This paper conducted an assessment of the directions followed by the research and innovation activities performed by Portuguese organisations in the fields encompassed by the "Blue Economy", at the light of national and EU strategies. The paper draws on an analysis of the projects developed by Portuguese actors in the context of European framework programmes to investigate: the areas that are being privileged and the role and positioning of different types of actors in the developments taking place. The results point to the emergence of new activities such as marine biotechnology and marine renewable industries, as well as the development of innovations in established industries exploiting marine living resources (fisheries and aquaculture). They likewise reveal that the research and technological activities towards the revitalisation of other established sea-related industries is still very limited. The results also highlight the prominent position of research organisations in both new and established areas. But they equally uncover the relevant position occupied by new technology intensive firms, particularly in areas that require the development of more application oriented methods, products, services, where they are often involved in tripartite relationships, intermediating between research and industrial application. Finally the results suggest that the international cooperation favoured by these projects permit to open-up the national system, contributing to broaden the organisations' knowledge bases and to extend their international networks.

Keywords: Blue economy · Innovation system · Research and innovation · New technology intensive firms · Sustainability · Portugal

1 Introduction

The "Blue Economy" was identified at EU level as a driver of European growth, through the development of new competences and activities that "harness the untapped potential

© Springer Nature Switzerland AG 2020
D. Rodionov et al. (Eds.): SPBPU IDE 2019, CCIS 1273, pp. 101–124, 2020.
https://doi.org/10.1007/978-3-030-60080-8_6

of Europe's oceans, seas and coasts for jobs and growth" while simultaneously striving to use the sea sustainably and "respect potential environmental concerns given the fragile nature of the marine environment" [10]. Strategies and policies were defined, to achieve these goals. Research and innovation, aiming at the revitalisation of established sectors and the development of emerging industries as well as at a better understanding of the marine environment and the requirements for its preservation were regarded as key elements in these strategies [10, 11].

EU level initiatives, namely the Integrated Maritime Policy for the European Union [11] and the Communication on Blue Growth [10], were translated into policy instruments. This is the case of funding instruments in the scope of the Framework Programmes, which shaped the R&D and innovation activities of a broad variety of actors that engaged in sea-related activities. The EU strategies and policies were also highly influential in policy formulation at the level of member-states. This was the case of Portugal that launched, in 2012, a revised National Ocean Strategy and Action Plan, whose model of development and areas of intervention were strongly influenced by the European framework.

The objective of the paper is to understand the influence of the EU and national strategies in the activities of the actors involved in the Blue Economy innovation system in Portugal. Therefore, the paper conducts an analysis of the directions followed by Portuguese organisations in the research and technology development activities conducted in the areas encompassed by the "Blue Economy", in order to understand:

a) which areas appear to be privileged, and the relative importance of new areas versus established ones;
b) the role and position of different types of actors in the developments taking place in the Blue Economy innovation system, namely the extent of firm involvement; and the role played by new technology intensive companies in developing new technologies and products and/or in linking between research and industrial activity.

The paper is structured as follows. Section 2 presents the concepts of Blue Economy and Blue Growth, identifies the strategies and policies that have been followed by the EU in the area and discusses how these initiatives can be understood in the context of the creation of a Blue Economy innovation system. Section 3 presents the development of the Blue Economy in Portugal, focusing on the public policies and strategies. Section 4 discusses the role that the several actors and their interaction can have in the building of the Blue Economy innovation system. The methodology used in the empirical analysis is presented in Sect. 5, while the results are presented in Sect. 6. Section 7 draws the main conclusion of the analysis.

2   The Blue Economy – A Policy-Driven Innovation System

The ocean provides a wide set of valuable natural resources, both renewable and non-renewable, which are used by several economic sectors [8, 25]. Over the last decades, the importance of these resources and the number and the activity of the sectors using them have increased [41]. At the same time, the sustainable use of ocean resources and the ecosystems integrity – namely environmental concerns with climate change and the overexploitation of natural resources [15] - are increasingly at the center of the strategies of both private and public actors involved in ocean-related activities [40].

In this context a new concept has emerged and gained momentum – the Blue Economy. Although it is not possible to find a consensual definition for this concept in the literature [43], there is agreement on the fact that it tries to address the economic activities related with a twofold perspective: the socio-economic development and expansion of sectors, and the achievement of the integrity and sustainability of ocean ecosystems [28, 43].

It is possible to identify several economic sectors involved in the Blue Economy. Although the sectoral classification varies by country and region [30, 35], the sectors involved in the Blue Economy usually have at least one of the following characteristics: are physically located in the ocean, use an ocean resource as an input in their production process, or are directly outputting goods or services to the ocean [30].

Along the concept of Blue Economy we can find the concept of "Blue Growth" that remits to strategies and public policies to promote the sustainable expansion of ocean-related economic activities in the marine and coastal environment [10] and their transformation through the development of new technologies and 'eco-innovation' [12, 13, 17].

This is the case of the European Union (EU), where, in 2007, a Communication from the European Commission (EC) recommended an Integrated Maritime Policy, setting the scene for the emergence and the sustainable development of marine-related activities [11]. This document addressed the conditions for the development of economic activities related to the sea – both established sectors and emerging industries – as well as the capacity to counteract the negative impacts of increased marine based activity on the quality of the marine environment, marine safety security and also the effects of climate change in oceans and coastal regions. This strategy would be anchored in excellence in marine research, technology and innovation.

Following this document, in 2012 the EC published a Communication on Blue Growth, defining a set of opportunities for marine and maritime sustainable growth, with a view to "place the blue economy firmly on the agenda of Member States, regions, enterprise and civil society" [10]. The document identifies the current key value-chains and activities and a set of new activities/sectors where targeted action could drive sustainable growth (e.g. blue energy and blue biotechnology), and proposes a number of initiatives to achieve this goal. Later, in 2014, it was complemented, by another Communication on Innovation in the Blue Economy that reinforced the role of research and innovation in the development of the blue economy while ensuring the protection of the marine environment and proposed additional actions to address the gaps in existing policies [12, 13].

The impact of these strategies and policies has been followed up by the Directorate-General for Maritime Affairs and Fisheries, which publishes an annual Blue Economy Report [14]. These documents contributed to establish a working definition of Blue Economy and its composition, which has been updated over time. According to the 2019 report the "EU's Blue Economy encompasses all sectoral and cross-sectoral economic activities related to the oceans, seas and coasts, including those in the EU's outermost regions and landlocked countries. This includes the closest direct and indirect support activities necessary for the sustainable functioning and development of these economic sectors within the single market. It comprises emerging sectors and economic value based on natural capital and non-market goods and services" [14].

Therefore, according to the EU perspective, the Blue Economy includes:

- Established traditional sectors, namely: Maritime transport; Coastal tourism; Marine living resources, extraction and commercialisation (fisheries, aquaculture; processing and distribution); Marine extraction of minerals, oil and gas; Ports, warehousing and water projects; Shipbuilding and repair.
- Emerging and innovative industries, namely: Blue energy (offshore wind energy; ocean energy); Blue bio economy; Marine minerals; Desalination; Maritime defence.
- Natural capital and ecosystem services.

The initiatives at EU level were reflected upon the design of the Framework Programme for Research and Innovation that was launched in 2014: the Horizon 2020. So it is to be expected that the areas of intervention defined as strategic received greater attention in the funding programmes, shaping the R&D activities of the actors' active in this domain and therefore contributing for the emergence of a new innovation system.

The innovation system literature considers that the construction of a new innovation system is a complex and gradual process along which the main components of the system – actors, networks and institutions – co-evolve [16]. This process involves a number of key functions [29], which include development of formal knowledge, direction of search, entrepreneurial experimentation, resource mobilization, materialization, market formation, legitimation, development of positive externalities.

In this approach innovation is conceptualized as a collaborative and distributed process, requiring the interaction between different actors, including firms and other organisations, such as universities and research centers, government agencies and industry associations, among others [16]. The institutional context where innovation unfolds is also central in the analysis, and includes the role of public policies in the field of innovation, particularly for the reorientation of innovation systems towards grand challenges, such as sustainability [6].

Innovation policies increasingly follow a system-centred approach [32], stimulating interaction between actors, interactive learning and cross-fertilisation. This entails collaboration processes between firms and other actors (e.g. research organisations), but also between firms with different characteristics and from different sectors [5, 18, 31].

3   Blue Economy in Portugal

Portugal is a maritime country with a large Atlantic continental coast that together with the two Archipelagos (Azores and Madeira) represent an exclusive economic zone with 1,72 million square kilometres. The country has historically engaged on sea-related activities. However, until recently some of the established marine sectors were struggling to adapt to structural changes and increased international competition; and the country was still underperforming in the emerging areas. Moreover, while there were some

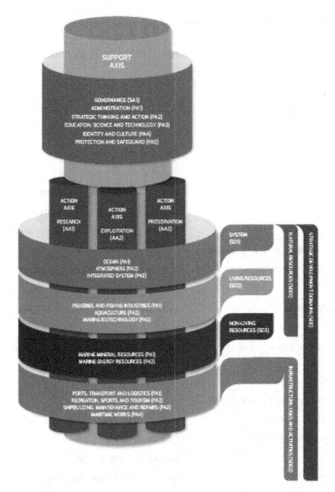

Fig. 1. Blue Economy strategic domains in Portugal [9]

organisations conducting marine research, the knowledge about marine ecosystems was regarded as insufficient to fully explore the sea resources and to address the environmental challenges that are increasingly central.

The Blue Economy EU strategies and policies had a strong impact upon the formulation of the Portuguese National Ocean Strategy 2013–2020. The political and financial relevance attributed to this area by the UE was regarded as an opportunity to formulate a strategy that enabled the country to recover the "national maritime identity" and regain a position in this area. This recovery translates into an increased contribution of maritime sectors to the domestic product, the strengthening of the scientific and technological capacity, and the stimulus to the development of new areas of action [38].

The strategy was operationalised by the Mar-Portugal Action Plan, which is organised along three Strategic Development Domains (SD), each including several Programme

Table 1. Blue Economy priority areas in European and Portuguese strategic documents

PLAN MAR PORTUGAL (DGPM, 2015)	BLUE ECONOMY REPORT (EU, 2019)	Type
SD1 – Governance		
Strategic thinking and action		
Education (ocean literacy)		N
Identity and culture		N
Protection & safeguard	Maritime Defence	N
SD2 – System		
Ocean	Natural capital and ecosystem services	NC
Atmosphere	Natural capital and ecosystem services	NC
Integrated system	Natural capital and ecosystem services	NC
SD3 - Natural resources: living resources		
Fisheries and fishing industries	Marine living resources - Fisheries	E
Aquaculture	Marine living resources - Aquaculture	E
Marine Biotechnology	Blue Bio economy	N
SD4 - Natural resources: non-living resources		
Marine mineral resources	Marine minerals & extraction of mineral, oil and gas	N&E
Marine energy	Blue energy	N
SD5 - Infrastructure, uses and activities		
Ports, transport & logistics	Ports, warehousing & maritime transport	E
Recreation, sports and tourism	Coastal tourism	E
Shipbuilding	Shipbuilding & repair	E
Maritime works	(Ports, … and) water projects	E

Source: Authors' own elaboration
Legend: E-established sectors; N – new industries; NC – new areas/natural capital

Areas (PA) (Fig. 1). It covers the main fields that compose the EU "Blue Economy" definition, with some adaptations to the country specificities. The programmes can include actions along one or more Axis: Research, Exploitation, and Preservation. The Plan also includes a Support Axis that includes several Programme Areas concerned with "Governance". Besides covering administrative issues and strategic issues, the Governance domain is also concerned with cultural issues, such as national identity and education, as well as with security.

Table 1 presents the main Programme Areas from Mar-Portugal Action Plan and relates them with the areas defined as strategic in EU Blue Economy policy documents. As becomes evident, there is strong overlap between them, even if there are some differences in thematic aggregation and sectoral organisation, reflecting the country specialisation.

Similarly to the European strategy, the Portuguese Strategy and the related Action Plan give a central role to research and innovation in the fulfilment of the goals established. The production of new scientific knowledge and the development of new technologies, products and services were seen as central to stimulate the creation of new industrial activities, to revitalise established industries and to tackle the environmental problems associated with increased human activity in the ocean environment. One of the goals of the Action Plan was to increase the participation of firms in these activities in order to strengthen the industrial structure around the "Blue Economy". This included the involvement of existing firms and the creation of new ones exploiting emerging technologies.

The Strategy and Plan have guided the sea-related activities conducted in Portugal. Following a period of some economic difficulties experienced by the country due to the financial crisis, it was revitalised and re-adjusted in 2015 [9]. Thus, the directions it establishes, namely in terms of areas of intervention to be privileged, are equally likely to have influenced the investment decisions of the Portuguese actors.

4   Actors and Networks in the Blue Economy Innovation System

As already pointed out the industrial activities encompassed by the Blue Economy include both established and new fields. Established sectors are mostly mature industries, while new technological advances often originate from outside the industry. Thus they may be related to activities conducted by research organisations or by new technology intensive firms (NTIFs), sometimes in partnerships with the potential users.

As already mentioned, the development of new activities and technologies has a central role in the industrial renewal of the Blue Economy and in promoting its sustainability. For this, research organisations and NTIFs tend to be key players. Research organisations are vital by performing their role as knowledge creators in the innovation system. NTIFs are young independent firms involved in the development and exploitation of new technological knowledge [19]. They can be particularly important in the Blue Economy since they often play a relevant part in the transformation of research results steaming from the academia in technologies, products and services, which are indispensable for the country to fully benefit from the R&D efforts. In fact, NTIFs often occupy an intermediate position between academic research and the market [4, 22] and create value in innovation systems, as agents of knowledge acquisition, transformation and diffusion [26, 36, 44].

Accordingly, research organisations and NTIFs are likely to be particularly active in the development of the new innovation system. Therefore, investigating the activity of these organisations, their relative positioning as well as their relationships – both between them and with existing companies from established sectors – are important to understand the dynamics of technological development in the field.

Relationships between these actors deserve a detailed analysis. Partnerships, namely collaborative R&D projects, have become a privileged instrument of firms in the development of new technologies. Through them, organisations share the risk and huge investments associated to the R&D process [24]. These collaborations are of utmost importance to small firms, which are unable to have in-house the various resources necessary for their activities. This is particularly the case of NTIFs, to whom competitiveness largely depends on the ability to quickly develop and renew the knowledge base, in order to generate a steady stream of innovations. Since knowledge is often complex and distributed, they need to rely extensively on relationships with other organisations [23, 33, 34]. But large and established firms are also intensively engaged in networking through collaborative R&D projects, in a world of increased specialization and distributed knowledge [3, 42]. Also, universities and research laboratories are very active in cooperating in R&D projects, not only with other academic partners, but also increasingly with the industry [37].

The objective of this paper is to conduct a first assessment of the directions followed by the research and technology development activities conducted by Portuguese organisations in the areas encompassed by the "Blue Economy", in order to understand:

a)   which areas appear to have been privileged and thus are likely to be developing faster; and namely the relative importance of new areas vs. advances targeting established ones;

b)   the role and position of different types of actors in the research activities conducted, namely to what extent they involve firms; and also, the role played by NTIFs in developing new technologies and products and/or in linking between research and industrial activity.

For this purpose, the paper analyses the research and technological development (RTD) activities conducted by Portuguese organisations in the context of European funded projects. The RTD Framework Programmes (FPs), launched in the early 1980s, are a major EU policy instrument, due to the vast budgets allocated to them. Collaborative research is highly supported by these multi-annual Programmes [1], stimulating research institutions, government agencies and industrial partners to cooperate in R&D projects and generating knowledge that spans across national borders. They are seen as pivotal for transforming nation-based research networks into formal collaboration arrangements between organisations at European level [27]. In the several FPs, collaborative research projects in both basic and applied research have been organized under broad thematic areas, such as Energy, ICT, Health, covering a wide range of the EU priorities [1].

While EU projects only correspond to a subset of the RTD activities potentially being conducted by Portuguese organisations, it can be argued that European programmes have nevertheless been a very important source of research funding. This was particularly so during part of the period under analysis, as the country was still in the aftermath of a financial crisis that hit Portugal strongly; and only recently there were conditions to increase national funding for RTD activities.

Thus, it can be assumed that the projects funded by European programmes offer a good overview of the areas where the most innovative Portuguese organisations decided to develop RTD activities. Thus they provide evidence of the areas being privileged, among the ones defined as priority by the public policy and enable us to start uncovering the influence of these policies in the research directions followed.

European projects, which in most programmes require multinational teams[1], also provide some information on the areas in which Portuguese organisations search for international partners or attempt to integrate international networks, and on the structure of these relationships thus offering some indications towards the transnational processes at work in the field.

5 Methodology

The paper focuses on the RTD activities conducted by Portuguese organisations in the context of projects funded under the most recent European Framework Programme for Research and Innovation: the Horizon 2020, active between 2014 and 2020. The Horizon 2020 operationalised some of Blue Growth strategic goals, particularly (but not exclusively) in the context of one of its Societal Challenges programmes - Food Security, Sustainable Agriculture and Forestry, Marine, Maritime and Inland Water Research and the Bioeconomy [13].

The research is based on all the projects with Portuguese participation funded since the beginning of the Programme (2014) until the end of 2018. In order to identify these projects a search was conducted in the database provided by the Community Research and Development Information Service (CORDIS) [https://cordis.europa.eu/projects/en] using a series of keywords related with the ocean and with sea-related activities and industrial sectors.

The projects obtained through this search were individually analysed in order to confirm whether they were effectively related to the Blue Economy themes and those unrelated were removed. As a result of this process we were left with 136 projects. For the projects selected we resorted again to the CORDIS database in order to collect information on the projects (Start date, End date, Overall budget, EU contribution, Objective, Coordinator and Participants) and on the participants (Type of organisation; Country; EU funding received).

Using the categories defined in the Portuguese Strategy and Action-Plan (Strategic Development Domains and Programme Areas presented in the first column of Table 1), the projects were subsequently classified according to the main area of activity.

The Portuguese organisations participating in these projects were also object of an additional treatment. NTIFs were singled out and distinguished from the remaining companies, since we intended to understand their role in the construction of a Blue Economy in Portugal.

To depict the system of relations emanating from the projects, a Social Network Analysis was performed. Collaborative projects constitute two-mode networks that link organisations to an event - the project. From these we extracted one-mode networks, considering inter-organisational networks, where a tie joins two organisations that collaborate in the same project. Symmetric adjacency matrices were built, valued by the number of common projects. Network diagrams were built using the NetDraw software.

---

[1] It should nevertheless be noticed that in Horizon 2020 some Programmes do not require those international partnerships and namely, that some are directed to individual firms (e.g. SME instrument) or researchers (ERC Grants). Thus, not all the projects analysed were composed of (international) teams.

6   Results

6.1   The Role and Position of Actors

The 136 projects with Portuguese participation that were identified as developing RTD activities related with the Blue Economy include both projects whose focus is exclusively in ocean related activities (78%) and a smaller number of projects whose activities have a broader scope and ocean is only one of the target areas (22%). A total of 33 projects were coordinated by Portuguese organisations. The network that reflects the system of collaborations emanating from these projects is depicted in Fig. 2.

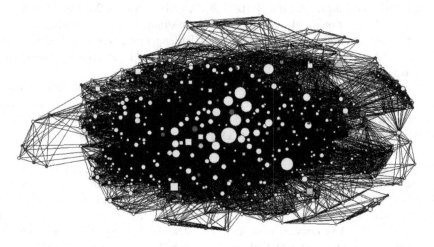

Fig. 2. Inter-organisational network considering all projects. Legend: Squares – Portuguese organisations; Circles – Foreign organisations; Red – Firms; Light Red – NTIFs; Yellow – Research Organisations; Blue – Public Organisations; Green – Other Organisations. The size of the node is proportional to the EU funding received by the organisation. (Color figure online)

These projects involve a total of 2279 participations from different types of organisations (Fig. 3), of which 226 are from Portuguese ones. Over half of the 226 Portuguese participations are from research organisations (ROs) and about 1/3 are from firms, the majority from NTIFs (Fig. 4). However, several organisations are involved in more than one project, which means that the number of organisations is lower than the number of participations in European projects. Considering the type of the 94 Portuguese organisations integrating the project teams, and classifying them by type, (Fig. 4), it is visible that the number of research organisations is similar to the number of firms and that, among the latter, NTIFs prevail over the other firms.

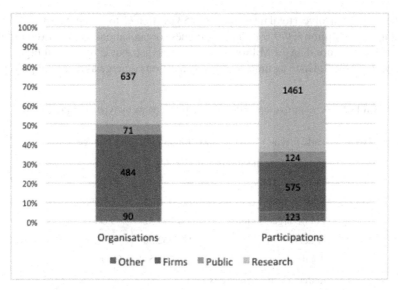

Fig. 3. Organisations and their participation in all projects. Source: Authors' own calculations.

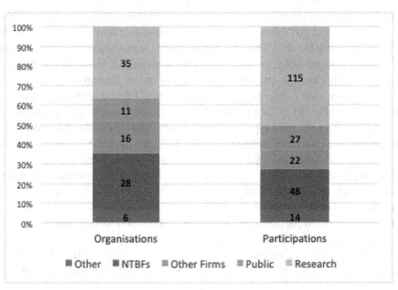

Fig. 4. Portuguese organisations and their participation in all projects. Source: Authors' own calculations.

The remaining participations are from public organisations (e.g. government departments or public agencies), corresponding to about 12% and from other types of organisations (e.g. associations and foundations), with a much lower weight (Figs. 3 and 4). Interestingly the relative weight of firm participations is higher than their expression in term of participant organisation.

The projects involve a total investment of 853 Million €, to which the EU contributed with almost 679 Million € (79,6%). The Portuguese organisations received a contribution from the EU of more than 73 Million €, which was distributed by type of organisation as shown in Table 2. Once again research organisations emerge as a central player.

Table 2. EU contribution to Portuguese participants by type of organization

Partner type	EU funding (€)	Percentage
Research organisations	6 710 568.80	51.4%
Firms – NTIF	20 904 288.90	9.2%
Firms – other	37 608 058.05	28.6%
Public organisations	7 004 129.32	9.6%
Others	947 662.50	1.3%
Total	73 174 707.57	100.0%

Source: Own calculations.

We have analysed the composition of project teams, in terms of Portuguese organisations. More than a half of the projects do not involve any Portuguese firm (Table 3). Considering those that do (Table 4), we found that mixed teams involving research organisations and firms are the most frequent. These mixed teams sometimes also encompass public or other organisations. Teams composed exclusively of research organisations or exclusively of firms are also present but are less frequent. Research organisations also sometimes partner with public or other organisations. Table 3 also shows the composition of teams where NTIFs are present: they are more frequently engaged with ROs and less frequently with other types of organisations. In some of these teams NTIFs are effectively part of tripartite relationships that include also other firms, namely firms from established sectors, to whom they are likely to act as knowledge intermediaries [7]. They are also engaged in individual projects, in the context of the SME instrument programme. It is also relevant to point out that, the 28 new technology intensive firms involved in these projects not only corresponded to 21.2% of the total of Portuguese project partners (68.5% of the firm partners) and to 29.8% of the individual organisations, but also coordinated 16 projects – corresponding to 48% of the Portuguese coordinators. This suggests that these firms effectively played an important role in the Blue Economy RTD activities being developed by Portuguese organisations in the context of EU projects.

Table 3. Project teams – involvement of Portuguese firms

Project team	Total projects	Percentage
Includes PT firms	57	41.9%
No PT firms	79	58.1%
Total	136	41.9%

Source: Authors' own calculations.

Table 4. Composition of Portuguese teams

Team	Total Number of projects	Including NTIFs Number of projects
RO only	16	
Firm only	13	13
R0 + Firm	41	13
RO + Public	07	
RO + Firm + Public	07	02
RO + Firm + Other	29	09
RO + Public + Other	05	
RO + Firm + Public + Other	18	04
Total	136	41

Source: Authors' own calculations.

It should nevertheless be noticed that the large majority of projects were composed of multinational teams, creating the conditions for international research cooperation. Only 20 projects involved exclusively Portuguese participants, in general one individual organisation, either a firm (13) or a research organisations (7). The international character of these collaborations is evident from the analysis of Fig. 5 that shows that Germany, Spain, France, the United Kingdom and Italy have an important participation in these projects. The centrality of foreign actors is also evident from the analysis of Fig. 1. Moreover, if we consider the top 10 organisation in terms of funding and participation in project (Tables 5 and 6) we see that the rankings are dominated by foreign organisations, which mostly are ROs.

While this may point to a lower relevance of Portuguese organisations in some of these projects and areas, it can also be regarded as an indicator of the efforts being conducted by several organisations to be part of the central RTD networks at work in some fields of the Blue Economy and to engage in the most advanced research being conducted in them at European level. The fact that 33 Portuguese organisations were coordinators of projects indicates that a few organisations have already gained enough competence and visibility to lead research in some of these areas.

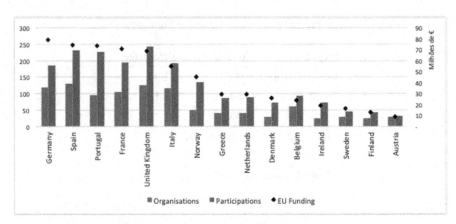

Fig. 5. Organisations, participations and funding by country – top 15 countries. Source: Authors' own calculations.

Table 5. Top 10 organisations in terms of funding

Organisation	Country	Type	Funding (€)
SENVION GMBH	Germany	Firm	12 236 926,11
INSTITUT FRANCAIS DE RECHERCHE POUR L'EXPLOITATION DE LA MER	France	Research	11 487 018,93
CENTRE NATIONAL DE LA RECHERCHE SCIENTIFIQUE CNRS	France	Research	10 967 341,39
EDP RENOVAVEIS SA	Spain	Research	9 829 783,38
HELLENIC CENTRE FOR MARINE RESEARCH	Greece	Research	8 857 187,54
CONSIGLIO NAZIONALE DELLE RICERCHE	Italy	Research	8 209 487,40
DANMARKS TEKNISKE UNIVERSITET	Denmark	Research	7 941 488,86
UNITED KINGDOM RESEARCH AND INNOVATION	UK	Research	7 591 401,25
AGENCIA ESTATAL CONSEJO SUPERIOR DE INVESTIGACIONES CIENTIFICAS	Spain	Research	6 734 511,72
FRAUNHOFER GESELLSCHAFT ZUR FOERDERUNG DER ANGEWANDTEN FORSCHUNG E.V	Germany	Research	6 610 803,75

Source: Authors' own calculations.

6.2   The Identification of Priority Areas

In order to understand the decisions of Portuguese organisations concerning the conduction of activities in the areas defined as priority in the Blue Economy strategies, we have

Table 6. Top 10 organisations in terms project participations

Organisation	Country	Type	Projects
INSTITUT FRANCAIS DE RECHERCHE POUR L'EXPLOITATION DE LA MER	France	Research	23
HELLENIC CENTRE FOR MARINE RESEARCH	Greece	Research	23
CONSIGLIO NAZIONALE DELLE RICERCHE	Italy	Research	21
AGENCIA ESTATAL CONSEJO SUPERIOR DE INVESTIGACIONES CIENTIFICAS	Spain	Research	21
CENTRE NATIONAL DE LA RECHERCHE SCIENTIFIQUE CNRS	France	Research	20
DANMARKS TEKNISKE UNIVERSITET	Denmark	Research	20
NATURAL ENVIRONMENT RESEARCH COUNCIL	UK	Research	16
UNITED KINGDOM RESEARCH AND INNOVATION	UK	Research	15
UNIVERSITETET I BERGEN	Norway	Research	15
MARINE INSTITUTE	Ireland	Research	13

Source: Authors' own calculations.

classified the projects according to the areas defined in the Portuguese strategy (presented in Table 1) and analysed each group in terms of number of projects, investment (project budget and EU contribution) (Table 7) and composition of the teams involved in the projects (Table 8). Network diagrams are also presented to support the analysis.

The analysis shows differences in what concerns the relative importance of the priority areas, as well as the position of different types of Portuguese organisations in them.

The System domain (SD2) is the most important in terms of investment and is also in the top in terms of number of projects, fact that is clearly visible in the size of the network (Fig. 6). In this domain the projects are mostly concerned with the ocean ecosystem and its interactions with other systems, focusing both on production of new knowledge about the marine environment, and on research on modes of monitoring, risk assessment and conservation. Therefore in this domain research is more focused on the sustainable oceans management than on the use of ocean resources. Considering the Portuguese actors, this domain is clearly dominated by research organisations, being the one with the largest share of teams not involving at least one firm (Table 7). This is also the domain with the highest share of projects involving tripartite teams (Research – Industry – Public /Other organisations), probably due to the fact that is dealing with the system. Some Portuguese firms – mostly NTIFs - appear in joint teams, as shown in the network diagram (Fig. 6) in activities concerned with monitoring services, namely firms active in the areas of instrumentation or marine robotics. Several foreign universities play a central role in this network.

Table 7. Relative weight of Blue Economy priority areas in EU projects with Portuguese participation

	Budget (%)	Funding (%)	No. projects (%)
SD 1 – Governance	12.3	10.8	15.4
Strategic thinking and action	4.7	3.2	5.1
Education (ocean literacy)	0.9	1.1	2.2
Identity and culture	0.9	1.1	2.9
Protection and safeguard	5.8	5.4	5.1
SD 2 – System	30.1	36.9	28.7
Ocean	13.8	17.0	15.4
Atmosphere	5.8	7.2	3.7
Integrated system	10.5	12.7	9.6
SD 3 – Natural resources: living resources	25.9	28.1	31.6
Fisheries and fishing industries	3.9	4.6	4.4
Aquaculture	6.3	7.5	7.4
Aquaculture and fisheries	1.5	1.7	1.5
Marine biotechnology	14.3	14.3	18.4
SD 4 – Natural resources: non-living resources	20.0	18.2	16.2
Marine mineral resources	0.2	0.3	0.7
Marine energy resources	19.7	17.9	15.4
SD 5 – Infrastructure, uses and activities	11.8	6.0	8.1
Ports, transport and logistics	7.7	2.6	2.2
Recreation, sports and tourism	0.0	0.0	0.0
Shipbuilding, maintenance and repairs	0.7	0.9	0.7
Maritime works	0.0	0.0	0.0
Several activities and marine energy	3.4	2.5	5.1
Total	100.0	100.0	100

Source: Authors' own calculations.

Research concerned with the exploitation of natural resources is also well positioned in terms of investment and number of projects (Table 6). The domain of Living Resources is the one that has the highest number of projects and is second in terms of investment. In this domain we find projects targeting both established and new activities. Projects targeting established activities – namely fisheries and aquaculture – have a lower weight than the ones targeting new activities – namely marine biotechnology. In fact, marine biotechnology appears as the most important programme area in terms of projects and the second in terms of investment. This may be explained by the large volume of investment made by the country in biotechnology in the last decades [2, 20]. Portuguese firms are present in several projects, as depicted in the network diagram (Fig. 7), often partnering with research organisations, but there is still a substantial number of projects, both in the new and in the established areas that only have Portuguese research organisations (Table 7). NTIFs are particularly important in marine biotechnology, where they seem to perform a bridging role among teams/projects. These firms also have some weight in aquaculture that is a still relatively new field in Portugal. A small group of Portuguese

Table 8. Composition of the project teams by Domain – percentage of the projects

Composition of the team	Governance (n = 18)	Living resources (n = 42)	Non-living resources (n = 22)	System level (n = 43)	Infrastructure, uses and activities (n = 11)	Total (n = 136)
Only ROs	22.2	16.7	4.5	4.7	18.2	11.8
Only Firms	0.0	14.3	13.6	2.3	27.3	9.6
ROs + Firms	11.1	23.8	50.0	37.2	18.2	30.1
ROs + Public/Other	22.3	4.8	9.0	9.3	0.0	8.8
ROs + Firms + Public/Other	44.4	40.4	22.7	46.5	36.4	39.7
Total	100	100	100	100	100	100

Source: Authors' own calculations.

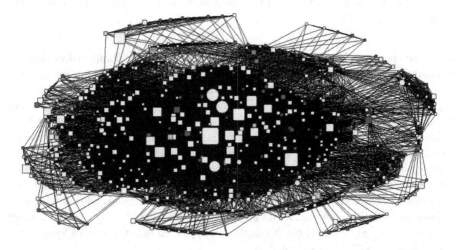

Fig. 6. Inter-organisational network – Projects in the System domain. Legend: Squares – Portuguese organisations; Circles – Foreign organisations; Red – Firms; Light Red – NTIFs; Yellow – Research Organisations; Blue – Public Organisations; Green – Other Organisations. The size of the node is proportional to the EU funding received by the organisation. (Color figure online)

established firms from the user sectors also participate in some teams. Foreign firms are particularly important in the established areas.

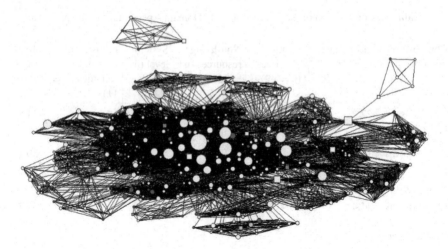

Fig. 7. Inter-organisational network - Projects in the Living Resources domain. Legend: Squares – Portuguese organisations; Circles – Foreign organisations; Red – Firms; Light Red – NTIFs; Yellow – Research Organisations; Blue – Public Organisations; Green – Other Organisations. The size of the node is proportional to the EU funding received by the organisation. (Color figure online)

The domain of Non-living Resources is almost exclusively composed of projects in marine energy, since the exploitation of mineral resources is a still underdeveloped area in Portugal. The focus is clearly on renewable energies, with oil and gas having a negligible position. This programme area is the one with the highest level of investment and the second in number of projects. This reflects the important activity that has been conducted by Portuguese organisations in marine renewables (wave and offshore wind energies) for several decades [21, 39]. This area combines projects that aim at the test of energy production prototypes, where firms appear alone or in partnership with research organisations; and projects that are concerned with the structuring of the field that tend to involve only research organisations. In the first case, partnerships can combine new technology intensive companies with large energy firms (both Portuguese and foreign as shown in Fig. 8). The network is clearly less populated than the ones of System and Living Resources domains shown above.

The Infrastructure, Uses and Activities domain is concerned with research targeting the other sea-related industries and has attracted the lowest number of projects and investment. Despite its potentially more application-oriented nature, there is still a few projects where the only Portuguese participants are research organisations (in some cases performing the role of bridges between teams/projects, as shown in Fig. 9). The exception are a set of projects with a broad scope whose results are relevant to any industrial activities located at sea and thus can be pertinent to the activities in this domain and to those in the area of marine energies. In this sub-set new technology intensive firms, namely firms active in new materials, have an important position. It is also worth noticing the absence of projects in the areas of Recreation, sports and tourism and of Marine Works.

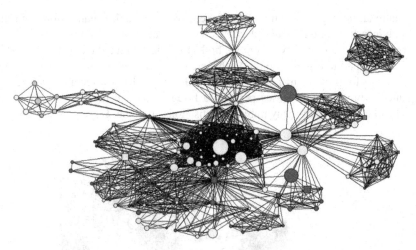

Fig. 8. Inter-organisational network - Projects in the Non-Living Resources domain. Legend: Squares – Portuguese organisations; Circles – Foreign organisations; Red – Firms; Light Red – NTIFs; Yellow – Research Organisations; Blue – Public Organisations; Green – Other Organisations. The size of the node is proportional to the EU funding received by the organisation. (Color figure online)

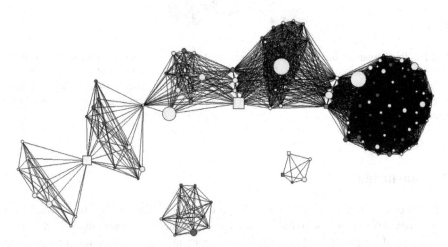

Fig. 9. Inter-organisational network - Projects in the Infrastructure, Uses and Activities domain. Legend: Squares – Portuguese organisations; Circles – Foreign organisations; Red – Firms; Light Red – NTIFs; Yellow – Research Organisations; Blue – Public Organisations; Green – Other Organisations. The size of the node is proportional to the EU funding received by the organisation. (Color figure online)

Finally, in the Governance domain (Fig. 10), it is possible to distinguish two main types of activities. One is concerned with cultural issues - the role played by the ocean in the national identity and the promotion of ocean literacy, which were important elements in the national strategy - where we find exclusively research organisations and also some public organisations, when it comes to Portuguese organisations. The other is concerned with ocean security, where we find a majority of mixed teams (research/firm and often also public organisations). In this area projects tend to involve development of instruments for monitoring and surveillance, developed by new technology intensive companies, which in some cases perform a bridging role in the network. It is also noticeable the presence of many public organisations and other type of organisations.

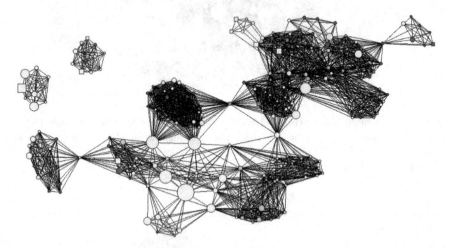

Fig. 10. Inter-organisational network - Projects in the Governance domain. Legend: Squares – Portuguese organisations; Circles – Foreign organisations; Red – Firms; Light Red – NTIFs; Yellow – Research Organisations; Blue – Public Organisations; Green – Other Organisations. The size of the node is proportional to the EU funding received by the organisation (Color figure online)

7   Conclusion

This paper conducted an assessment of the directions followed by the research and technology development activities conducted by Portuguese organisations in the areas encompassed by the "Blue Economy" – an emergent innovation system that is being policy-driven, both at European and national levels. More specifically the paper addressed the areas that are being privileged and the position of different types of actors in the developments taking place. For this purpose, the paper analysed the research and technological development (RTD) activities conducted by Portuguese organisations in in the context of projects funded by the most recent European Framework Programme, the Horizon 2020, between 2014 and 2018.

   The results indicate an important investment, in particular by research organisations, towards the increase of the sustainability of ocean-related activities, in what can be described as system structuring activities. This encompasses the development of knowledge about the marine resources and marine environment, as well as on the impacts of human activity and ways to reduce or remediate them. This area has been identified as a gap in the national strategy and is a critical step in the sustainable exploitation of the ocean.

The results also indicate that, so far, activities targeting industrial activity are mostly concentrated in the exploitation of living resources and in marine energies. In the first case, by attempting to revitalise established industries – fish capture and transformation – that have a long tradition in the country, namely through research investment in aquaculture. But also by investing strongly in a new area – marine biotechnology – whose activities target a variety of potential application sectors (e.g. fisheries, agrofood, health, cosmetics, environment), with a important component of activities whose goal is to upgrade established industries or increase their sustainability. In the second case, by strengthening the investment made in marine renewable energies by the country, in the last decades. The results also suggest that some areas are still attracting less attention: the principal gaps appear to be the limited activities targeting other sea-related industries, such as shipbuilding or ports and marine transportation that also have an important weight in the country economy, and the absence of activity in the area of marine mineral resources.

Concerning the role and positioning of the several types of organisations, the results show the central role of research organisations that not only dominate in more structural activities but are often part of mixed teams in more application-oriented projects. They also point to an important role of new technology intensive companies, active in areas with a higher technological intensity (such as biotechnology, instrumentation, underwater robotics and materials) and in areas that require development of more application oriented methods, products, services. These companies often perform the role of intermediaries between research organisations and other firms. A similar role is played in some areas by a few other technology-oriented companies, either large firms or firms belonging to large groups, as is the case of the marine energy area (non-living resources). These two types of firms are often part of mixed teams with research organisations and, in a few cases, also with established companies from user sectors. But there is a very limited participation of this latter group in the projects related to their area of activity.

The analysis was mostly focused on Portuguese organisations. However, the majority of the projects also involve organisations from other countries. In fact, the main actors in these projects, both in terms of received funding and in terms of participation in projects, are foreign organisations. In this broader context, where mixed teams – involving firms and research organisations – were frequent, Portuguese organisations could also profit from the interaction with reputed foreign partners, namely in areas where new competence was being acquired. Thus, the areas targeted by these projects were also the areas where the development of country capabilities in the Blue Economy fields could reap the benefits from international research cooperation, which potentially contributed to broadening knowledge bases and extending international networks.

These results can be relevant for policy makers, providing some indications on the relative success of the strategies and policy instruments devised to develop a Blue Economy in Portugal and signalling the areas that may still require greater attention.

This research can be expanded in three different ways. Firstly, it is possible to extend the analysis to the projects funded at national level, which may provide additional insights into the activities of organisations that may not have the capacity to successfully apply to European projects (which have very high requirements), but can also play a role in the development of the Blue Economy in Portugal. Secondly, it is possible to perform a more detailed analysis of the contents and outcomes of the projects funded, in order to gain a deeper understanding of the areas being targeted and the advances achieved. Finally, it is possible to do a more detailed analysis of the interactions between different areas, as well as the potential sectoral interactions and cross-fertilization the projects may enable. In particular, this would allow to understand the part played by the new areas in the development of established industries, which is one important objective of the Blue Growth strategy.

References

1. Amoroso, S., Coad, A., Grassano, N.: European R&D networks: a snapshot from the 7th EU Framework Programme. Econ. Innov. New Technol. **27**(5–6), 404–419 (2018)
2. Arantes-Oliveira, N.: A case study on obstacles to the growth of biotechnology. Technol. Forecast. Soc. Chang. **74**(1), 61–74 (2007)
3. Arora, A., Gambardella, A.: Evaluating technological information and utilizing it: Scientific knowledge, technological capability, and external linkages in biotechnology. J. Econ. Behav. Organ. **24**(1), 91–114 (1994)
4. Autio, E.: New, technology-based firms in innovation networks symplectic and generative impacts. Res. Policy **26**(3), 263–281 (1997)
5. Bergek, A., Jacobsson, S., Carlsson, B., Lindmark, S., Rickne, A.: Analyzing the functional dynamics of technological innovation systems: a scheme of analysis. Res. Policy **37**(3), 407–429 (2008)
6. Cagnin, C., Amanatidou, E., Keenan, M.: Orienting European innovation systems towards grand challenges and the roles that FTA can play. Sci. Public Policy **39**(2), 140–152 (2012)
7. Conceição, O., Sousa, C., Fontes, M.: Research-based spin-offs as knowledge conveyers in innovation networks. In: Bernhard, I. (ed.) Innovation, Entrepreneurship and Industrial Dynamics in Internationalized Regional Economies. Universit, Trollhättan (2017)
8. Costanza, R.: The ecological, economic, and social importance of the oceans. Ecol. Econ. **31**(2), 199–213 (1999)
9. DGPM: O Plano Mar Portugal – Anexo B - Actualização 2015 (2015). https://docs.wixstatic.com/ugd/eb00d2_7c89d6cb1c534720873df9c2cfa8d14d.pdf
10. EC: Blue Growth opportunities for marine and maritime sustainable growth Communication from the Commission to the European Parliament, the Council, the European Economic and Social Committee and the Committee of the Regions (COM/2012/0494 final) (2012)
11. EC: An Integrated Maritime Policy for the European Union. Communication from the Commission to the European Parliament, the Council, the European Economic and Social Committee and the Committee of the Regions – (COM(2007) 574 final) (2007)
12. EC: Innovation in the Blue Economy: realising the potential of our seas and oceans for jobs and growth. Communication from the Commission to the European Parliament, the Council, the European Economic and Social Committee and the Committee of the R (2014)
13. EC: HORIZON 2020 in brief The EU Framework Programme for Research & Innovation, Luxembourg: Publications Office of the European Union (2014)
14. EC: The EU Blue Economy Report. 2019. Publications Office of the European Union. Luxembourg (2019)
15. Ecorys: Blue Growth - Scenarios and Drivers for Sustainable Growth from the Oceans, Seas and Coasts. Ecorys, Rotterdam, Brussels (2012)

16. Edquist, C.: Systems of Innovation: Technologies, Institutions, and Organizations. Pinter, London (1997)
17. EU: Directive 2014/89/EU - Maritime Spatial Planning. Off. J. Eur. Union 135–145 (2014)
18. Fiore, A., Grisorio, M.J., Prota, F.: Regional innovation systems: which role for public policies and innovation agencies? Some insights from the experience of an Italian region. Eur. Plan. Stud. **19**(8), 1399–1422 (2011)
19. Fontes, M., Coombs, R.: Contribution of new technology-based firms to the strengthening of technological capabilities in intermediate economies. Res. Policy **30**(1), 79–97 (2001)
20. Fontes, M., Sousa, C.: Types of proximity in knowledge access by science-based start-ups. Eur. J. Innov. Manage. **19**(3), 298–316 (2016)
21. Fontes, M., Sousa, C., Ferreira, J.: The spatial dynamics of niche trajectory: the case of wave energy. Environ. Innov. Soc. Transitions **19**, 66–84 (2016)
22. Fontes, M.: The process of transformation of scientific and technological knowledge into economic value conducted by biotechnology spin-offs. Technovation **25**(4), 339–347 (2005)
23. Hagedoorn, J., Link, A.N., Vonortas, N.S.: Research partnerships. Res. Policy **29**(4–5), 567–586 (2000)
24. Hagedoorn, J.: Inter-firm R&D partnerships: an overview of major trends and patterns since 1960. Res. Policy **31**(4), 477–492 (2002)
25. Hallwood, P.: Economics of the Ocean: Rights, Rents, and Resources. Routledge, Abingdon (2014)
26. Harrison, R.T., Leitch, C.: Voodoo institution or entrepreneurial university? Spin-off companies, the entrepreneurial system and regional development in the UK. Reg. Stud. **44**(9), 1241–1262 (2010)
27. Heller-Schuh, B., et al.: Analysis of Networks in European Framework Programmes (1984–2006) (No. JRC63467). JRC Scientific and Technological Reports, Europea (2011)
28. Howard, B.C.: Blue growth: stakeholder perspectives. Mar. Policy **87**, 375–377 (2018)
29. Jacobsson, S., Bergek, A.: Innovation system analyses and sustainability transitions: contributions and suggestions for research. Environ. Innov. Soc. Transitions **1**, 41–57 (2012)
30. Klinger, D.H., Eikeset, A.M., Davíðsdóttir, B., Winter, A.M., Watson, J.R.: The mechanics of blue growth: management of oceanic natural resource use with multiple, interacting sectors. Mar. Policy **87**, 356–362 (2018)
31. Malhotra, A., Schmidt, T.S., Huenteler, J.: The role of inter-sectoral learning in knowledge development and diffusion: Case studies on three clean energy technologies. Technol. Forecast. Soc. Chang. **146**, 464–487 (2019)
32. Nauwelaers, C., Wintjes, R.: Towards a new paradigm for innovation policy. In: Asheim, B., Isaksen, A., Nauwelaers, C., Tödtling, F. (eds.) Regional Innovation Policy for Small-Medium Enterprises, pp. 193–220. Edward Elgar, Cheltenham (2003)
33. Owen-Smith, J., Powell, W.W.: Knowledge networks as channels and conduits: the effects of spillovers in the Boston biotechnology community. Organ. Sci. **15**(1), 5–21 (2004)
34. Ozman, M.: Inter-firm networks and innovation: a survey of literature. Econ. Innov. New Technol. **18**(1), 39–67 (2009)
35. Park, D., Seo, K., Kildow, D., Judith, T.: Rebuilding the classification system of the ocean economy. J. Ocean Coastal Econ. **2014**(1), 4 (2014)
36. Perez, M.P., Sánchez, A.M.: The development of university spin-offs: early dynamics of technology transfer and networking. Technovation **23**(10), 823–831 (2003)
37. Perkmann, M., Walsh, K.: University–industry relationships and open innovation: Towards a research agenda. Int. J. Manage. Rev. **9**(4), 259–280 (2007)
38. RCM: Resolução do Conselho de Ministros no 12/2014 – Estratégia Nacional para o Mar 2013–2020 (Nacional Ocean Strategy 2013–2020) Diário da República, 1.a série, N.o 30, 12 de fevereiro de 2014 (2014)

39. Sarmento, A., Rocha, A.B., Morais, T.: Offshore Renewable Energy - Current Status. Future Perspectives For Portugal, INEGI (2014). http://www.inegi.up.pt/publicacoes//livros/pdf/Off shore_Renewable_Energy.pdf
40. Silver, J.J., Gray, N.J., Campbell, L.M., Fairbanks, L.W., Gruby, R.L.: Blue economy and competing discourses in international oceans governance. J. Environ. Dev. 24(2), 135–160 (2015)
41. Stefanovic, T.A., Farmer, C.J.Q.: The development of world oceans & coasts and concepts of sustainability. Mar. Policy 42, 157–165 (2013)
42. Veugelers, R., Cassiman, B.: R&D cooperation between firms and universities. Some empirical evidence from Belgian manufacturing. Int. J. Ind. Organ. 23(5), 355–379 (2005)
43. Voyer, M., Quirk, G., McIlgorm, A., Azmi, K.: Shades of blue: what do competing interpretations of the Blue Economy mean for oceans governance? J. Environ. Plann. Policy Manage. 20(5), 595–616 (2018)
44. Walter, A., Auer, M., Ritter, T.: The impact of network capabilities and entrepreneurial orientation on university spin-off performance. J. Bus. Ventur. 21(4), 541–567 (2006)

Regional Industrial Specialization: Case of Russian Electrical Equipment, Electronic and Optical Equipment Industry

Angi Skhvediani$^{(\boxtimes)}$ ⓘ, Tatiana Kudryavtseva ⓘ, and Dmitrii Rodionov ⓘ

Peter the Great St. Petersburg Polytechnic University, Saint Petersburg, Russia
{shvediani_ae,kudryavtseva_tyu,drodionov}@spbstu.ru

Abstract. Development of the digital economy affects numerous structural elements of socio-economic systems. A feature of the evolving Information and Communications Technology (ICT) industry is its contribution to the economic growth of regions. It is expected that development of this industry has to generate positive effects for a region. It is assumed that the focus of regions on the ICT industry will lead to their economic growth. The authors test this assumption on the example of Russia's regions. To do this, the authors differentiated a manufacturing sector of the ICT industry - Electrical equipment, electronic and optical equipment industry, and analyzed specialization of regions in the industry within the period 2009–2018. Then the authors built up panel spatial models to evaluate direct and indirect effects of specialization of regions' productivity. The analysis results showed that spatial Marshall–Arrow–Romer (MAR) spillover effects and direct MAR effects of employee location turned out to be significant and positive. However, direct MAR effects of sales revenue location and spatial MAR spillover effects of wage location proved to be negative, which can make assumptions about availability of Jacob and Porter positive effects. The obtained results can be used to develop a regional and interregional industrial policy in the framework of supporting the ICT industry in Russia. Further trends of research can be focused on measuring Jacobs and Porter effects for the ICT industry in Russia.

Keywords: Regional industrial specialization · MAR spillover effects · ICT industry · Externalities

1 Introduction

Development and dissemination of digital technologies lead to changes in numerous elements of the socio-economic system [1–3]. In particular, ICT evolution results into modifications of business models of companies [4, 5], financial organizations [6], development vectors in education [7, 8]. Apart from this, it is common to highlight cumulative effects of ICT dissemination at the level of regions [9]. Digitalization is specifically regarded as a source of regions' economic growth [10]. It is assumed that the economic growth is achieved through intensification of innovative activity [11] in regions, which

© Springer Nature Switzerland AG 2020
D. Rodionov et al. (Eds.): SPBPU IDE 2019, CCIS 1273, pp. 125–139, 2020.
https://doi.org/10.1007/978-3-030-60080-8_7

are ready to adopt ICT [12], or where the ICT industry is concentrated [13, 14]. Therefore, regional industrial specialization can be considered as a source of economic growth in the conditions of digitalization.

The impact of the ICT industry on the economic growth is studied quite well on a global scale. For instance, it has been proved that economic growth and an amount of investments into the ICT industry are correlated in such countries as Korea [15, 16], India [17], China [18], USA [19] etc.

The ICT industry is regarded as one of the most promising industries In Russia [20, 21]. Hence ICT evolution is associated with the development of knowledge economy [22, 23] and with the source of Russia's economy modernization [24, 25]. However, empirical research, which would prove the presence of spillover effects of the ICT industry for Russia's regions, is poorly available. On top of this, there is no research devoted to analysis of an essential manufacturing component of the ICT industry - Electrical equipment, electronic and optical equipment industry. This sphere is a core of the ICT industry, as it deals with manufacturing the equipment that will be used for transition to Industry 4.0.

According to this, the goal of the research is to analyze regional industrial specialization of Russian regions in the Electrical equipment, electronic and optical equipment industry, and to evaluate interrelations between development of this activity and indices of the economic growth in 2009–2018.

In order to achieve the set goal, the following tasks were solved.

1. The authors determined indices of regional industrial specialization which could be used for analysis of Electrical equipment, electronic and optical equipment industry in Russian regions.
2. Two versions of the Russian statistical classifier of economic activities were compared, the old one (OKVED OK 029-2001) valid till July 10, 2016, and a new version of the classifier OKVED-2 (OK 029-2014) valid from July 11, 2016, to collect comparable data about development of the ICT industry in Russia in the period 2009–2018.
3. The authors calculated and analyzed indices of regional industrial specialization of regions in the Electrical equipment, electronic and optical equipment industry in Russia within the period 2009–2018.
4. The authors made an analysis of spatial dependencies between indices of regions' specialization in the Electrical equipment, electronic and optical equipment industry in Russia, and indices of economic growth. There were evaluated spatial Marshall–Arrow–Romer (MAR) spillover effects and direct MAR effects for specialization of regions in the Electrical equipment, electronic and optical equipment industry.

2   Literature Review on Foundations of Regional Industrial Specialization

Studying MAR, Jacobs and Porter externalities, measuring their effect on regional and industrial indices are a rather popular trend of research in the field of spatial economy [26, 27].

The concept of Marshall–Arrow–Romer (MAR) externalities arose as a result of formalization [28] of research results [29–31]. In the framework of the MAR concept it is assumed that high concentration of an industry in a region leads to intensification of knowledge spillovers between companies, and to stimulation of innovations in it. Namely, specialization of a region in a certain activity results to development of intra-industry and intra-cluster externalities depending on a level of aggregation and a type of information organization.

On the other hand, Jacobs theory implies that sources of externalities outside the respective industry or cluster in a region are most important. Thus, it is diversity of knowledge sources, i.e. diversity of industries presented in the region, that ensures higher qualitative and quantitative characteristics of knowledge spillover, and consequently, leads to intensification of innovative activity in the respective regional industry [32].

The concept of Porter's externalities is generally close to the idea of Jacobs, it supports the statement that competition contributes to economic growth [33]. According to Porter's theory, market competition is a single reason for companies to start innovations and to increase productivity [34]. From Porter's standpoint, the best exchange of knowledge is between companies located in the same vertically integrated industry [35]. Therefore, knowledge spillover is likely to occur in concentrated industries, rather than geographically isolated businesses. Thereby industry concentration should make a positive effect on its growth [36]. In this regard, Porter's externalities are closer to MAR externalities.

The given research is devoted to analysis of regions' specialization in a certain industry. Therefore, we test available MAR externalities positive for regions, which result from location of the Electrical equipment, electronic and optical equipment industry. Presumably, if available MAR effects are positive, indices of regional specialization in a certain activity will be positively related to the index of economic growth. Consequently, if specialization of neighboring regions is positively related to the index of economic growth, positive spillover effects will occur.

3 Methodology and Data

The ICT sector considered in this research is presented by its manufacturing part. Table 1 shows comparison of activities by OKVED and OKVED-2. This comparison is needed, as from 2017 companies have to submit reports by a new structure of activity types. Therefore, it is essential to match data by different codes to obtain comparable results for the period 2009–2018.

Table 2 presents data downloaded for the analysis. The data were collected from the web-site of the Unified Interagency Information Statistical System. The data are divided into two groups. The first is a core group, it is used to calculate indices of regional industrial specialization. These data were classified in accordance with Table 1. Sales revenue data and average wage data were transformed into fixed prices of 2009. The second group shows additional indices, it is used to calculate control variable models.

In order to calculate specialization indices, Location Quotients (LQ) will be used [37, 38]. LQ shows how many times the ratio of employees is higher in the region's activity under study, than the ratio of employees in the same activity all over the country.

Table 1. Comparison of OKVED and OKVED -2 codes

OKVED	OKVED – 2
Section DL Production of electrical equipment, electronic and optical equipment	• Production of PCs, electronic and optical equipment • Production of electrical equipment • Production of other finished goods

Table 2. Input data

Variable	Variable type	Definition
E_{igt}	Core	Number of employees in industry i of region g per year t, people
S_{igt}	Core	Sales revenue in industry i of region g per year t, mln. rubles in fixed prices of 2009
W_{igt}	Core	Average wage in industry i of region g per year t, rubles in fixed prices of 2009
cr_{gt}	Additional	Number of crimes in region g per year t, cases
$lexp_{gt}$	Additional	Life expectancy in region g per year t, years
$unem_{gt}$	Additional	Unemployment rate in region g per year t, %
$chim_{gt}$	Additional	Infant mortality, deaths per 1000 live births

In terms of this research the following LQs are calculated:

$$E_{igt}^{LQ} = \frac{E_{igt}}{E_{gt}} / \frac{E_{it}}{E_t} \tag{1}$$

$$S_{igt}^{LQ} = \frac{S_{igt}}{S_{gt}} / \frac{S_{it}}{S_t} \tag{2}$$

$$W_{igt}^{LQ} = \frac{W_{igt}}{W_{gt}} / \frac{SW_{it}}{W_t} \tag{3}$$

where:

- E is a number of employees, people;
- S is sales revenue, million rubles in fixed prices of 2009;
- W is wage, rubles in fixed prices of 2009;
- i is an index for an industry;
- g is an index for a region;
- t is an index for a year;
- LQ is an index for location quotient.

LQ, calculated by employment, is a common measurement unit to assess specialization of a region [39–41]. This index reflects available critical mass of an industry in a region under study [42, 43]. However, LQ, calculated by sales revenue and wage tends to be unavailable in the research [36]. From the authors' standpoint, this shortcoming is crucial, as the above-mentioned indices allow evaluating not only parameters of regional specialization related to a relative concentration of employment, but parameters of specialization related to a relative concentration of sales revenue and wage. For instance, a region can have a relatively low concentration of employment, but a relatively high concentration of sales revenue and wage. This can be a sign of high-productivity industry in this territory. Consequently, inclusion of additional location indices ensures deeper analysis of regional industrial specialization.

As the index of economic growth, the authors use labor productivity, which is calculated as sales revenue in a region divided by a number of employees in the region:

$$prod_{gt} = \frac{S_{gt}^{LQ}}{E_{gt}^{LQ}} \tag{4}$$

MAR externalities will be measured using econometric methods. In particular, five types of the models, presented in Table 3, will be evaluated.

Table 3. Specification of the models

Type of model	Equation
Pooled model	$lnprod_{gt} = \alpha i_N + \beta_1 E_{igt}^{LQ} + \beta_2 S_{igt}^{LQ} + \beta_3 W_{igt}^{LQ} + \gamma_k X_t + \varepsilon_t$
Random effects model	$lnprod_{gt} = \alpha i_N + \beta_1 E_{igt}^{LQ} + \beta_2 S_{igt}^{LQ} + \beta_3 W_{igt}^{LQ} + \gamma_k X_t + u_t$ $u_t = \mu + \varepsilon_t$
Fixed effects model	$lnprod_{gt} = \alpha i_N + \beta_1 E_{igt}^{LQ} + \beta_2 S_{igt}^{LQ} + \beta_3 W_{igt}^{LQ} + \gamma_k X_t + \mu + \varepsilon_t$
Spatial random effects model	$lnprod_{gt} = \delta W lnprod_{gt} + \alpha i_N + \beta_1 E_{igt}^{LQ} + \beta_2 S_{igt}^{LQ} + \beta_3 W_{igt}^{LQ} + W E_{igt}^{LQ} \theta_1$ $+ W S_{igt}^{LQ} \theta_2 + W W_{igt}^{LQ} \theta_3 + \gamma_k X_t + u_t$ $u_t = \lambda W u_t + \mu + \varepsilon_t$
Spatial fixed effects model	$lnprod_{gt} = \delta W lnprod_{gt} + \alpha i_N + \beta_1 E_{igt}^{LQ} + \beta_2 S_{igt}^{LQ} + \beta_3 W_{igt}^{LQ} + W E_{igt}^{LQ} \theta_1$ $+ W S_{igt}^{LQ} \theta_2 + W W_{igt}^{LQ} \theta_3 + \gamma_k X_t + \mu + u_t$ $u_t = \lambda W u_t + \varepsilon_t$

Prefix *ln* defines a natural logarithm of a variable.

i_N is a vector of ones associated with the constant term parameter α.

X_t is a matrix of control variables essential to explain region – level differences between the panels. Control variables are presented by a natural logarithm of infant mortality in a region, a natural logarithm of life expectancy, and an unemployment rate.

W is a matrix of return distances, which is applied to evaluate the effect of neighboring regions. Using it, we can measure not only availability of direct effects (MAR externalities), but indirect effects (spillover effects from industry localization/MAR spatial spillover effects).

4   Results and Discussion

4.1   Analysis of Employment Specialization

In general, throughout the Russian Federation a number of employees in the Electrical equipment, electronic and optical equipment industry reduced from 824,214 people in 2009 to 744,655 in 2018, i.e. by 10.3% for a decade.

Within the period 2009–2018 only 22 regions showed a positive increase in employees (Fig. 1), which confirms availability of centers where the critical mass of an activity grows. Leading regions by an absolute increase in employment for a decade are the following: Moscow region (+9,236 people; +22%); Kostroma region (+8,775 people; +800%), Saint Petersburg (+3,779 people; +6%), Leningrad region (+3,360 people; + 88%), Ryazan region (+2,871 people; +18%).

Fig. 1. Increase in an absolute number of employees in the Electrical equipment, electronic and optical equipment industry in Russia's regions in 2018 compared to 2009, people.

53 regions had a reduction of employment, which means that the critical mass of the activity under study fell. The greatest decline in a number of employees by an absolute value for a decade was in the following regions: Moscow (−19,239 people; −19%), Sverdlovsk region (−13,757 people; −34%), Vladimir region (−9,198 people; −34%), Khanty-Mansi Autonomous district-Yugra (Tyumen region) (−7,094 people; −87%), the Republic of Bashkortostan (−6,624 people; −38%), and Samara region (−6,549 people; −36%).

In four regions an activity is unavailable, namely in the following: the Republic of Ingushetia, the Republic of Tyva, Chukotka Autonomous District, Nenets Autonomous District (Arkhangelsk region).

Figure 2 and Fig. 3 show location of employees in the Electrical equipment, electronic and optical equipment industry in 2009 and 2018 respectively. Location, or relative concentration of employees, rose in 31 regions. Differences which concern an increase in employees are related to the fact that LQ is a relative index. Consequently, in several regions LQ rose, as a number of employees in the Electrical equipment, electronic and optical equipment industry fell at a slower pace than average throughout the region.

Fig. 2. Location of employees in the Electrical equipment, electronic and optical equipment industry in Russia's regions in 2009

Fig. 3. Location of employees in the Electrical equipment, electronic and optical equipment industry in Russia's regions in 2018

Leaders by a growth in the location of employees for a decade have been the following: Kostroma region (+2.90), the Mari El Republic (+1.39), the Chuvash Republic (+.93), Ryazan region (+.81), the Udmurt Republic (+.590).

Among the leaders by a decrease in the location of employees in the Electrical equipment, electronic and optical equipment industry one can point out the following regions: Vladimir region (−.56), Kabardino-Balkarian Republic (−.55), Khanty-Mansi Autonomous district-Yugra (Tyumen region) (−.53), Kaluga region (−.48), Sverdlovsk region (−.39).

4.2 Analysis of Sales Specialization

On the whole, in the Russian Federation the sales revenue in the Electrical equipment, electronic and optical equipment industry at fixed prices of 2009 rose from 840,062 to 151,0447 million rubles, which accounted for 80%.

Within the period 2009—2018, 57 regions saw a positive growth in sales revenue (Fig. 4), which proves availability of centers, where the critical mass of an activity increases. For a decade leaders by an absolute growth of sales have been: Moscow (+118,817 mln rubles; +70%), Saint Petersburg (+90,074 mln rubles; +100%), Moscow region (+3,779 people; +6%), Leningrad region (+3360 people; +88%), Ryazan region (+2871 people; +18%).

26 regions had a decrease in sales revenue, which means that the critical mass of the activity under study reduced. The greatest decline in sales revenue by an absolute value for a decade was seen in the following regions: Khanty-Mansi Autonomous district -Yugra (Tyumen region) (−5,838 mln rubles; −76%), Kaliningrad region (−4,497 mln

Fig. 4. Growth in sales revenue in the Electrical equipment, electronic and optical equipment industry in Russian regions in 2018 compared to 2009, million rubles in fixed prices of 2009.

rubles; −24%), the Republic of Dagestan (−2,122 mln rubles; −74%), Yamalo-Nenets Autonomous district (Tyumen region) (−1,694 mln rubles; −99%), Khabarovsk region (−1,323 mln rubles; −83%).

Figure 5 and Fig. 6 show location of the sales revenue in the Electrical equipment, electronic and optical equipment industry in 2009 and 2018 respectively. The location, or a relative concentration, of the sales revenue grew in 31 regions.

For this decade the leaders by a growth in the location of sales revenue are the following regions: Kostroma region (+6.18), the Chuvash Republic (+3.14), Ulyanovsk region (+1.70), Kirov region (+1.45), Lipetsk region (+1.44).

Fig. 5. Location of sales revenue in the Electrical equipment, electronic and optical equipment industry in Russian regions in 2009

Fig. 6. Location of sales revenue in the Electrical equipment, electronic and optical equipment industry in Russian regions in 2018

The leaders by a decline in the location of sales revenue in the Electrical equipment, electronic and optical equipment industry can be listed the following: Kaliningrad region (−3.85), Kabardino-Balkarian Republic (−3.83), Kaluga region (−3.77), the Republic of Dagestan (−3.43), Pskov region (−2.77).

4.3 Analysis of Wage Specialization

Generally, in the Russian Federation the average wage in the Electrical equipment, electronic and optical equipment industry at fixed prices of 2009 grew from 17,334 rubles to 24,670 rubles, which accounted for 42%.

Within the period 2009–2018, 63 regions showed a positive growth of wage (Fig. 7). Among the leaders by an absolute growth of wage for this decade one can point out the following: Astrakhan region (+29,993 rubles; +216%), Moscow (+18,061 rubles; + 81%), Ulyanovsk region (+16,894 rubles; +200%), Kamchatka region (+15,461 rubles; +54%), Kaluga region (+14,880 rubles; +125%).

Fig. 7. Growth in average wage in the Electrical equipment, electronic and optical equipment industry in Russian regions in 2018 compared to 2009, rubles in fixed prices of 2009.

Figure 8 and Fig. 9 show the location of wage in the Electrical equipment, electronic and optical equipment industry in 2009 and 2018 respectively. The location, i.e. a relative concentration of wage, rose in 34 regions.

For this decade the leaders by a growth in the location of wage are the following regions: Astrakhan region (+1.43), Ulyanovsk region (+0.77), the Mari El Republic (+0.47), Kaluga region (+0.93), Penza region (+0.31).

Fig. 8. Location of wage in the Electrical equipment, electronic and optical equipment industry in Russian regions in 2009

The leaders by a decline in the location of wage in the Electrical equipment, electronic and optical equipment industry can be listed the following: Jewish Autonomous region (−0.95), Lake Baikal region (−0.95), Republic of Khakassia (−0.94), Magadan region (−0.61), Altai Republic (−0.50).

Fig. 9. Location of wage in the Electrical equipment, electronic and optical equipment industry in Russian regions in 2018

4.4   Evaluation of Interrelation Between Specialization of Russian Regions in the Electrical Equipment, Electronic and Optical Equipment Industry and Their Economic Growth

Table 4 presents results of regression modeling of interrelations between specialization of Russian regions in the Electrical equipment, electronic and optical equipment industry and labor productivity.

Evaluation of spillover effects for a productivity level and random changes in productivity of neighboring regions is positive and significant. It is implied that regions with high productivity are located close to highly productive regions, whereas regions with low productivity are located near lowly productive ones. Besides, in case random positive changes in productivity occur in a region, the neighboring regions will have positive productivity effects too, and vice versa.

Location of sales revenue in the Electrical equipment, electronic and optical equipment industry is negatively related to average labor productivity in regions. This confirms that regional specialization on «electrical equipment, electronic and optical equipment» can have a negative effect on the general productivity of a region. In other words, specialization on this production output generates negative MAR externalities for a region, rather than positive ones. This proves availability of positive Jacobs and Porter externalities, i.e. a positive effect of diversification in a region at the expense of knowledge exchange between industries. The estimates of spatial MAR spillover effects of sales revenue location turned out to be insignificant, at the level 0.05.

Table 4. Evaluation of interrelation between specialization of Russian regions in the Electrical equipment, electronic and optical equipment industry and labor productivity

Regressor	Estimated models						
	Pooled model	FE model	RE model	Spatial FE model	Spatial RE model	Spatial FE model with instruments	Spatial RE model with instruments
S^{LQ}_{igt}	−0.037*	−0.023**	−0.024**	−0.025***	−0.026***	−0.028***	−0.031***
	(0.014)	(0.008)	(0.008)	(0.007)	(0.007)	(0.007)	(0.007)
E^{LQ}_{igt}	0.044	0.062*	0.055	0.057*	0.047	0.083**	0.084**

(continued)

Table 4. (*continued*)

	(0.034)	(0.031)	(0.030)	(0.028)	(0.027)	(0.029)	(0.028)
w_{igt}^{LQ}	−0.631***	0.065*	0.040	0.044	0.050	0.032	0.023
	(0.070)	(0.030)	(0.032)	(0.028)	(0.028)	(0.028)	(0.028)
$lnchim_{gt}$	−0.274***	0.194***	0.157***	0.077*	0.061*	0.071*	0.061*
	(0.059)	(0.028)	(0.030)	(0.030)	(0.030)	(0.030)	(0.030)
$lncr_{gt}$	0.283***	0.161***	0.227***	0.076	0.144***	0.076	0.158***
	(0.020)	(0.037)	(0.032)	(0.041)	(0.037)	(0.042)	(0.037)
$lnlexp_{gt}$	2.128***	9.020***	8.391***	6.446***	6.068***	5.978***	5.606***
	(0.466)	(0.351)	(0.357)	(0.488)	(0.497)	(0.510)	(0.474)
$unem_{gt}$	−0.075***	−0.005	−0.012***	0.010**	0.009**	0.010**	0.007*
	(0.005)	(0.003)	(0.003)	(0.003)	(0.003)	(0.003)	(0.003)
i_N	−9.991***	−40.207***	−38.034***		−27.357***		−25.184***
	(2.033)	(1.653)	(1.652)		(2.180)		(2.091)
$Wlnprod_{gt}$				0.434***	0.416***	0.381***	0.452***
				(0.087)	(0.082)	(0.108)	(0.091)
Wu_t				0.664***	1.362***	0.758***	0.741***
				(0.090)	(0.087)	(0.069)	(0.068)
WS_{igt}^{LQ}						−0.067	−0.077
						(0.056)	(0.054)
WE_{igt}^{LQ}						0.619*	0.820***
						(0.281)	(0.201)
WW_{igt}^{LQ}						−1.078***	−1.182***
						(0.302)	(0.239)
σ_e				0.118***	0.118***	0.116***	0.117***
				(0.003)	(0.003)	(0.003)	(0.003)
σ_u					0.535***		0.492***
					(0.045)		(0.042)
Number of observations	790	790	790	790	790	790	790
Number of panels		79	79	79	79	79	79
Wald test of spatial terms (chi2)				110.363	247.047	191.792	166.512
Wald test of spatial terms (p)				0.000	0.000	0.000	0.000
AIC	898.232	−1044.866	–	−986.719	−672.841	−997.450	−692.206
BIC	935.608	−1007.490	–	−939.999	−616.776	−936.713	−622.126
log-likelihood	−441.116	530.433	–	503.360	348.420	511.725	361.103

Stars refer to the significance level of the coefficients: * for $p < .05$, ** for $p < .01$, and *** for $p < .001$

Standard errors in parentheses

Employment location in the Electrical equipment, electronic and optical equipment industry is positively related to average labor productivity in regions in spatial models with instruments. This claims that a relative concentration of employees in the Electrical equipment, electronic and optical equipment industry can have a positive effect on the general productivity of a region. It is implied employment specialization in this industry can generate positive MAR externalities for a region. The estimates of spatial MAR spillover effects of employment location prove to be considerable, which means that the employment location in the Electrical equipment, electronic and optical equipment industry in neighboring regions is positively connected with their average labor productivity.

Location of wage in the Electrical equipment, electronic and optical equipment industry in regions of the Russian Federation does not have a statistically significant relation with the index of average labor productivity in regions in spatial models. However, the estimates of spatial MAR spillover effects of employment location proved to be considerable. The employment location in the Electrical equipment, electronic and optical equipment industry in neighboring regions is negatively connected with their average labor productivity. Therefore, regions with higher average wage in the Electrical equipment, electronic and optical equipment industry border on regions with lower productivity. Thereby MAR spillover effects tend to be negative, i.e. highly productive regions will border on regions where average wage in the Electrical equipment, electronic and optical equipment industry is low, and vice versa.

Thus, it is possible to draw a conclusion that the tested assumption about the fact that regional specialization in the Electrical equipment, electronic and optical equipment industry is positively related to their economic growth, is only partly true. Namely, spatial MAR spillover effects and direct MAR effects of employment location proved to be significant and positive. However, direct MAR effects of sales revenue location, and spatial MAR spillover effects of wage location turned out to be negative, leading to the conclusion about availability of positive Jacobs and Porter effects.

5 Conclusion

We analyzed regions of the Russian Federation specialized on the Electrical equipment, electronic and optical equipment industry. The analysis of specialization was conducted by using both indices of absolute growth for a decade and indices of a relative concentration of employment, sales revenue and average wage. We identified the regions with the greatest growth and greatest reduction of the critical mass and average wage in the industry.

Then, with the methods of spatial econometrics we tested the assumption about availability of positive MAR externalities of regional specialization on a manufacturing component of the ICT industry - Electrical equipment, electronic and optical equipment industry. The assumption was partly verified, as we found out the presence of significant positive spatial MAR spillover effects and direct MAR effects for location of employees. However, direct MAR effects of sales revenue location and spatial MAR spillover effects of wage location proved to be negative, which could imply availability of positive Jacobs and Porter effects. Therefore, we can draw a conclusion that it is not definitely confirmed that the relation between the region's specialization on the ICT industry and its economic growth is positive.

The practical contribution of the research is based on the identification of regions specialized in the Electrical equipment, electronic and optical equipment industry, with the analysis of dynamics of particular specialization indices. Consequently, the results of the research can be used to develop a regional and interregional policy targeted at the support of the ICT industry in Russia.

Further trends of the research can be aimed at measuring Jacobs and Porter externalities and spillover effects for regions' economies. In addition, it is expedient to continue developing methodology for analysis of regional industrial specialization. Another trend of the research can be related to complex classification of regions based on specialization indices, which can help systemize the results of the analysis on various aspects of regional industrial specialization.

Acknowledgements. The reported study was funded by RFBR, project number 19-310-90069.

References

1. Fareri, S., et al.: Estimating industry 4.0 impact on job profiles and skills using text mining. Comput. Ind. **118**, 103222 (2020)
2. Aptekman, A., et al.: Digital Russia: new reality, p. 133 (2017)
3. Kudryavtseva, T., Skhvediani, A., Arteeva, V.: Theoretical analysis on the effect of digitalization on the labor market. In: Proceedings of the European Conference on Knowledge Management, ECKM 2019, vol. 1, p. 672–679 (2019)
4. Bouwman, H., et al.: The impact of digitalization on business models. Digit. Policy Regul. Gov. **20**(2), 105–124 (2018)
5. Verevka T.V.: Digital transformation of enterprises of the hospitality industry: global experience and prospects. In: Proceedings of the 33rd International Business Information Management Association Conference, pp. 629–640 (2019)
6. Bataev, A.V., Plotnikova, E.V.: Assessment of digital banks' performance. Espacios **40**(20), 24 (2019)
7. Plotnikova, E.: Digitalization of education in the leading universities of Saint Petersburg. In: IOP Conference Series: Materials Science and Engineering, vol. 497, no. 1, p. 12047. IOP Publishing (2019)
8. Plotnikova, E.V., Efremova, M.: Digitalization as a trend: points of growth for Russian universities - participants of the "5-100-2020" program. In: Proceedings of the 33rd International Business Information Management Association Conference, pp. 800–808 (2019)
9. Liao, Y., et al.: The impact of the fourth industrial revolution: a cross-country/region comparison. Prod. SciELO Brasil **28**, 1–18 (2018)
10. Vasetskaya, N., Gaevskaia, T.: Digitalization as an instrument for economic growth. In: Proceedings of the 33rd International Business Information Management Association Conference, pp. 8914–8919 (2019)
11. Babskova, O., Nadezhina, O., Zaborovskaya, O.: Innovative activities in a region in the conditions of the development of the digital environment. Int. J. Innov. Technol. Explor. Eng. **8**(12), 4361–4365 (2019)
12. Degtereva, V.A., Ivanov, M.V., Barabanov, A.A.: Issues of building a digital economy in modern Russia. In: European Conference on Innovation and Entrepreneurship, pp. 246–253. Academic Conferences International Limited (2019)
13. Kurikka, H., Kolehmainen, J., Sotarauta, M.: Path development and constructed regional resilience: the case of the Nokia-led ICT industry in Tampere. Tampereen yliopisto (2017)

14. Baypinar, M.B.: Evolution of ICT and software industry: crisis, resilience and the role of emerging clusters. In: 56th Congress of the European Regional Science Association: "Cities & Regions: Smart, Sustainable, Inclusive?", 23–26 August 2016, Vienna, Austria, pp. 1–13. European Regional Science Association (ERSA), Louvain-la-Neuve (2016)
15. Hong, J.: Causal relationship between ICT R&D investment and economic growth in Korea. Technol. Forecast. Soc. Change **116**, 70–75 (2017)
16. Heo, P.S., Lee, D.H.: Evolution of the linkage structure of ICT industry and its role in the economic system: the case of Korea. Inf. Technol. Dev. **25**(3), 424–454 (2019)
17. Erumban, A.A., Das, D.K.: Information and communication technology and economic growth in India. Telecomm. Policy **40**(5), 412–431 (2016)
18. Li, Y., Lee, S.-G., Kong, M.: The industrial impact and competitive advantage of China's ICT industry. Serv. Bus. **13**(1), 101–127 (2019). https://doi.org/10.1007/s11628-018-0368-7
19. Min, Y.-K., Lee, S.-G., Aoshima, Y.: A comparative study on industrial spillover effects among Korea, China, the USA, Germany and Japan. Ind. Manag. Data Syst. **119**(3), 454–472 (2019)
20. Zemtsov, S., et al.: Potential high-tech clusters in Russian regions: from current policy to new growth areas. Foresight STI Gov. **10**(3), 34–52 (2017)
21. Lazanyuk, I., et al.: IT industry as a prerequisite for digital economy (Cases of Russia and India). In: Proceedings of the 5th International Multidisciplinary Scientific Conference on Social Sciences and Arts SGEM, no. 3 (2018)
22. Larin, S.M., Baranova, N.M., Khrustalev, E.Y.: Development of the IT-industry as a growth trend in the knowledge economy: analyzing the evidence from the USA and Russia. Natsional'nye Interes. prioritety i Bezop. Natl. Interes. Priorities Secur. **13**(4), 615–630 (2017)
23. Kudryavtseva, T.J.T.J., Skhvediani, A.E.A.E., Bondarev, A.A.A.A.: Digitalization of banking in Russia: overview. 2018 International Conference on Information Networking (ICOIN), Chiang Mai, pp. 636–639. IEEE (2018)
24. Mechitov, A., Moshkovich, E.: IT industry as a driving force in modernizing Russian economy. Calif. Bus. **4**(1), 29–34 (2016)
25. Popkova, E.G., Sergi, B.S.: Will industry 4.0 and other innovations impact Russia's development. Explor. Futur. Russ. Econ. Mark. Towar. Sustain. Econ. Dev. 51–68 (2018)
26. Beaudry, C., Schiffauerova, A.: Who's right, Marshall or Jacobs? The localization versus urbanization debate. Res Policy. **38**(2), 318–337 (2009)
27. Bavina, K.: New economic geography: agglomeration and spatial concentration. In: SSRN, pp. 44–47 (2016)
28. Shleifer, A., et al.: Growth in cities. J. Polit. Econ. 100(6), 1126–1152 (1992)
29. Marshall, A.: Principles of Economics, vol. 1. Macmillan London (1890)
30. Arrow, K.J.: Economic welfare and the allocation of resources for invention. In: Rowley, C.K. (eds.) Readings in Industrial Economics. Palgrave, London (1962). https://doi.org/10.1007/978-1-349-15486-9_13
31. Romer, P.M.: Increasing returns and long-run growth. J. Polit. Econ. **94**(5), 1002–1037 (1986)
32. Jacobs, J.: The Economies of Cities. Random House, New York (1969)
33. Sörensson, R.: Marshallian sources of growth and interdependent location of Swedish firms and households. Department of Economics (2010)
34. Porter, M.E.: Competitive advantage, agglomeration economies, and regional policy. Int. Reg. Sci. Rev. **19**(1–2), 85–90 (1996)
35. De Lucio, J.J.: The effects of externalities on productivity growth in Spanish industry. Reg. Sci. Urban Econ. **32**, 241–258 (2002)
36. He, C., et al.: Economic transition, dynamic externalities and city-industry growth in China. Urban Stud. **47**(1), 121–144 (2010)

37. Haig, R.M.: Major Economic Factors in Metropolitan Growth and Arrangement: A Study of Trends and Tendencies in the Economic Activities Within the Region of New York and Its Environs. Arno Press, Regional Survey (1974)
38. Kopczewska, K., et al.: Measuring Regional Specialisation: A New Approach, p. 487. Palgrave Macmillan, Cham (2017). https://doi.org/10.1007/978-3-319-51505-2
39. Rodríguez-Pose, A., Comptour, F.: Do clusters generate greater innovation and growth? An analysis of European regions. Prof. Geogr. **64**(2), 211–231 (2012)
40. Schepinin, V., Skhvediani, A., Kudryavtseva, T.: An empirical study of the production technology cluster and regional economic growth in Russia. In: Amorim, M.P.C., Costa, C., Au-Yong-Oliveira, M. (eds.) Proceedings of the European Conference on Innovation and Entrepreneurship, ECIE, pp. 732–740. Academic Conferences and Publishing International Limited (2018)
41. Morrissey, K.: A location quotient approach to producing regional production multipliers for the Irish economy. Pap. Reg. Sci. **95**(3), 491–506 (2016)
42. Ketels, C., Protsiv, S.: European cluster panorama. Cent. Strateg. Compet. Stock. pp. 1–69 (2014). https://cluster.hse.ru/mirror/pubs/share/215584354
43. Lindqvist, G.: Disentangling clusters (2009)

Response of an Educational System and Labor Market to the Digital-Driven Changes in the Economic System

The Methodological Features of the Economic Evaluation of Personnel Management Operational Projects

Alexander Bril[1] ⓘ, Olga Kalinina[1] ⓘ, Sergey Barykin[1](✉) ⓘ, and Anna Burova[2] ⓘ

[1] Peter the Great St. Petersburg Polytechnic University, Polytechnicheskaya, 29, 195251 St. Petersburg, Russian Federation
olgakalinina@bk.ru

[2] Financial University Under the Government of the Russian Federation (Moscow) St. Petersburg Branch, Syezhinskaya Str., 15-17, 197198 St. Petersburg, Russian Federation

Abstract. Undoubtedly, the organizations need to be flexible and able to continuously improve business processes with the relevant measures intended for organizing staff. The purpose of the research is to propose methodology for economic evaluation of operational projects of personnel management based at crises enterprises on the mechanism for making managerial decisions on the effective systems of remuneration in a digital environment. The authors' studies have shown that when enterprises are withdrawn from crisis situations, operational projects are mainly implemented, not investment ones. This fully applies to personnel management projects. The important thing here is that the funds for their implementation are significantly limited, and there are a lot of options for such projects when developing enterprise development plans. A feature of operational projects is that they are usually financed from funds from the company's turnover; accordingly, they need a quick return, i.e. minimum payback. Personnel management operational projects could be defined as diverse and multidirectional regarding automation and staff planning, determining the need for hiring personnel, selecting and hiring employees, their training and adaptation, organizing career opportunities, attesting and evaluating the performance of job functions, motivation, employee incentives, organizing payments and labor rationing. This list of elements of the personnel management system can be supplemented and expanded. Therefore, the selection of the most effective projects for crisis enterprises requires a methodology for economic evaluation of just such operational projects to improve personnel management system. The proposed methodology for economic evaluation of operational projects of personnel management of different organizations and enterprises includes three main types of work, including localization of the project with the advantages and disadvantages of events being identified, as well as the establishment and calculation of criteria for cost and effectiveness of measures for the company as a whole, and, finally, the development of a mechanism and quantitative calculation of changes in risks in the enterprise.

Keywords: Human resource management · Personnel management · Remuneration · Crisis management · Digital environment · Economic evaluation · Human capital

© Springer Nature Switzerland AG 2020
D. Rodionov et al. (Eds.): SPBPU IDE 2019, CCIS 1273, pp. 143–154, 2020.
https://doi.org/10.1007/978-3-030-60080-8_8

1 Introduction

With the modern world being digital organizations become flexible and continuously improving business processes. Undoubtedly, strategically important for any company is an appropriate system of personnel management. One of the most common causes of the bankruptcy of companies is inefficient decisions of managers in difficult market situations. The bankruptcy procedures imposed by the arbitral tribunal are primarily based on the selection of the arbitration manager. We suggest to identify three main blocks of organizational and economic problems of crisis management:

– staff;
– accounting, analytics, and planning;

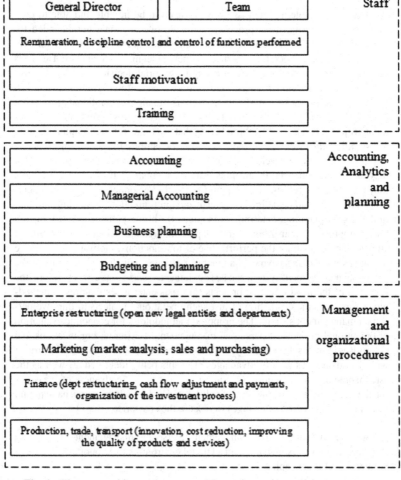

Fig. 1. The composition and content of the main work on crisis management

– management and organizational procedures (Fig. 1).

In addition to the staff structure, the communication must be very well developed. Thus, the purpose of our research is to propose methodology for economic evaluation of operational projects of personnel management based at crises enterprises on the mechanism for making managerial decisions on the effective systems of remuneration in a digital environment.

2 Materials and Methods

The decision making providing a competitive advantage in crises aims to integrating human resources into a business strategy [12, 13], and the effectiveness of such complex decisions depends on human resource management taking into the account the features of crisis. The theory and practice of overcoming crisis in enterprises was considered in various scientific papers [1, 3, 19]. Crises affecting humans, their communities and organizations could be treated in terms of external and internal factors (in relation to the company), and one of the most important reason of the crisis is the personnel competence level, i.e. decision making for the crisis management being the main aspect of human resource development [7, 26]. In the paper [4] the default risk of the financial institution's liability structure is analyzed. Some researchers consider and financial system systemic risk in view of the issue asset diversification [18, 27]. Some economists showed such reason of crisis as leveraging by banks [10]. Others investigate factors influencing the strategy process [30]. The findings indicate that various rewards techniques are useful, such as both a grading system and the development of key performance indicators [22]. It should be noted that the coordination of management efforts towards improving the economic situation is important as well as communications between employees within the company [14, 21].

In [9] the scientists study the organizational culture regarding crisis management. Undoubtedly the personnel management system could be treated as the most important [13]. The ability of the personnel management system to mobilize staff to overcome difficulties is based on the innovations [23, 24]. The Model of Crisis prevention being studied in [17] considers the synergy of both Quality Management Principles and Risk Management Principles which should be used in the economic evaluation of personnel management operational projects.

The competitive advantage in the digital economy assumes that personnel knowledge enables employees develop their skills [15]. The remuneration of personnel should be based on the reliable information and organizational capabilities [23], and human resources becomes a key asset in the modern world [26]. The organizational and managerial capabilities for innovation being analyzed by the system of indicators of external financial analysis are studied in [13]. Such indicators are divided into two groups: the appraisal of the financial stability and the assessment of the business activity.

Lin Y, Wang X, Xu R suggest interesting method of human resource allocation based on the cloud environment [16]. We could agree with the point of view that contemporary requirements exceed the possibilities of traditional competitive human resource allocation. So, Lin Y, Wang X, Xu R prove that auto-encoder neural network-based method in the cloud environment should improve the effectiveness of human resource management and the degree of matching between jobs and staffs due to a semi-automatic manner of human resource allocation [16]. The abovementioned method is based on deep learning architecture in the business process by using appropriate cloud resources (Fig. 2).

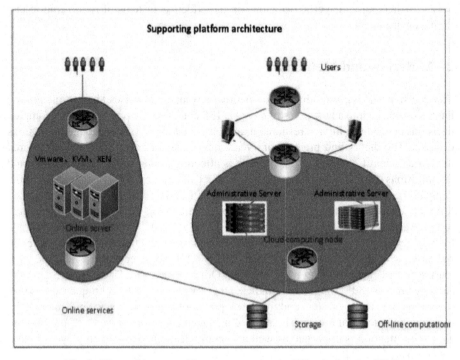

Fig. 2. The architecture of human resource scheduling in the cloud [16]

Taking into account the similarities and deep presentation between staff modules enables both modeling of semi-automatic human resource allocation process and facilitating optimized personnel position matching and effectively enhance the efficiency of personnel management [16]. Some other methods have made great achievements in human resource scheduling by cloud environment such as personnel allocation strategies and mechanisms in the field of business process management research studied by Boon C, Eckardt R, Lepak DP, Boselie P [4]. They show that it should be analyzed resource-based view (RBV) in strategic management enabling to identify firm resources in reliance with the basic criteria of the RBV (valuable, rare and imitable). Chen M, Leung considers cognition-based communications with a new architecture that includes two layers as follows: the communication layer and cognition layer (Fig. 3), consisting of two core cognitive engines, i.e., the resource cognitive engine and data cognitive engine [8]. Cognitive computing can be used for network analytics, network applications, and network automation. Network analytics include cognitive analytics in networking and network problem diagnosis through machine learning [8]. Network application includes resource allocation for virtualized networks using machine learnings, energy-efficient network operations via machine learning algorithms, and machine learning algorithms for network security. Network automation includes deep learning and reinforcement learning in network control and management, and predictive and self-aware networking maintenance [8].

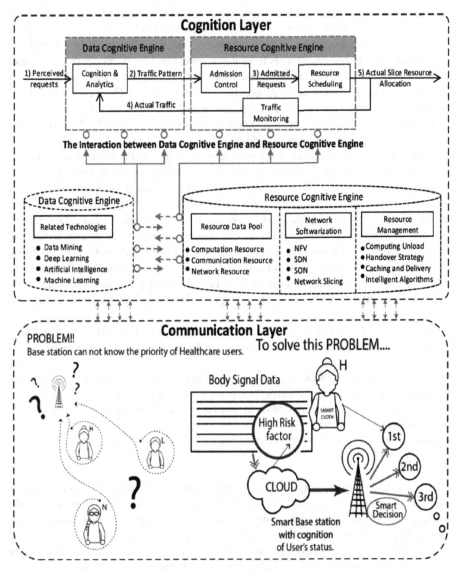

Fig. 3. The architecture of cognition-based communications [8]

The importance of deploying IoT of mobile nodes into healthcare is described by Oueida S, Kotb Y, Aloqaily M (i.e., medical team and stuff) is adopted in order to improve the system and thus leads to a better allocation of resources and an enhancement in performance measures [20]. E Silva LC and Costa APCS propose a framework based on dynamic programming with a methodology that determines the fit between the complete set of skills available from a candidate member of a project team and the skills required for that project so as to assist the process of allocating human resources in information system projects [11]. No doubt, Project Managers should ensure that the project appropriately receives staff with the required skills at the right time [11]. To do so, there is a need to find the professionals in the organization who have the profile needed and are available from the moment that the project needs them. Moreover, there is also the need to allocate, in the best possible way, professionals to projects which are already underway and either require more staff with the same skills or one or more team members who have the skills required for the phase of the project that is about to begin. This task is not simple, because usually there are a number of different possible allocations [11].

Based on the provisions of the well-known methodology UNIDO for the commercial evaluation of projects [2], which includes two stages (economic and financial analysis), the authors have developed and tested a one-stage methodology for the economic analysis of operational personnel management projects. Focusing on the above requirements when creating the methodology, an order and criteria were developed to assess the impact of the project on labor productivity and profit growth of the company in question, profitability of sales and assets, level of production and operational risks. Operational projects are distinguished by short terms of implementation and insignificant investment costs, financed from the own funds of enterprises. It is essential for them to establish, as a result of the implementation of the personnel management project, opportunities to reduce the current costs of enterprises and generate additional profit, increase profitability and manageability of the company, and change the level of production and commercial risks.

The proposed methodology for economic evaluation of operational projects of personnel management of existing enterprises includes three main types of work:

- localization of the project, to identify the advantages and disadvantages of events, centers for reducing and increasing costs, areas of growth and risk reduction,
- the establishment and calculation of criteria for cost and effectiveness of measures for the company as a whole,
- development of a mechanism and quantitative calculation of changes in risks in the enterprise.

The methodology for localizing personnel management projects is considered in [5]. The purpose of localization is to single out a personnel management project for the necessary work, results and costs from the entire company management system, from its constantly ongoing operational and investment projects. The issues of risk assessment based on the mechanism of operational leverage (leverage) during the implementation of the PMC projects were also considered in earlier works of the authors [6].

3   Results

The authors' studies have shown that when enterprises are withdrawn from crisis situations, operational projects are mainly implemented, not investment ones. This fully applies to personnel management projects. The important thing here is that the funds for their implementation are significantly limited, and there are a lot of options for such projects when developing enterprise development plans. A feature of operational projects is that they are usually financed from funds from the company's turnover; accordingly, they need a quick return, i.e. minimum payback. Therefore, the selection of the most effective projects for crisis enterprises requires a methodology for economic evaluation of just such operational projects to improve personnel management in existing enterprises. Moreover, in conditions of digitalization of the economy, the main requirements for such a methodology are the clarity and simplicity of the criteria for making effective decisions, the use of available accounting and management information of the enterprise for calculations, and the relative simplicity of the calculations.

In the present article, we will dwell in more detail on the selection of criteria-based indicators of the effectiveness of operational projects of personnel management system as well as both the procedure for their calculation and decision-making. Operational projects for personnel management of enterprises are diverse and multidirectional. The most common among them are the following: automation and staff planning, determining the need for hiring personnel, selecting and hiring employees, their training and adaptation, organizing career opportunities, attesting and evaluating the performance of job functions, motivation, employee incentives, organizing payments and labor rationing. This list of elements of the personnel management system can be supplemented and expanded. From the point of view of economic assessment, it is necessary to divide them into three groups according to their target orientation:

- elements on the improvement of which depends only on the growth of sales volumes of products;
- elements, investments in which only affect the reduction of labor costs, the number of personnel and, accordingly, current costs, production costs;
- elements of the personnel management system that affect both the reduction of current costs and the growth in sales volumes.

For example, the work to motivate and stimulate the personnel of the sales department or open independent centers for special training are aimed at increasing sales volumes and company profits. On the other hand, automation of work in production units and training of personnel to perform new functions mainly affect the reduction in the number of employees, growth of labor productivity and reduction of current costs of the enterprise. Table 1 illustrates the economic performance indicators of operational projects of the personnel management system projects of different target orientation and the procedure for their calculation.

A study of the implementation of personnel management projects showed that their economic efficiency depends on the target orientation and the real structure of the cost of sales of the enterprise. Personnel management system projects aimed at increasing sales volumes in companies with a low share of variable costs have a greater effect on generating additional profit and increasing labor productivity than those associated only with a reduction in the number of employees. Enterprises with a high level of variable costs and relatively low fixed costs have a different picture. Here, projects aimed at reducing the number of staff are more cost-effective.

Table 1. Settlement procedure and economic performance indicators of personnel management system projects of different target areas

The main objectives of the personnel management project	Procedure and economic performance indicators of personnel management system projects	Economic performance indicators and assessment criteria
Growth in sales and cash receipts of the enterprise	1. Calculation of sales volumes of products and current costs for the enterprise development project, taking into account the share of fixed costs 2. Localization and refinement of the project technology 3. Calculation of project costs and increase in fixed costs of the enterprise 4. The definition of additional profit from sales for the company and the assessment of payback 5. Calculation of project-specific criteria-based performance indicators	- the number, volume of sales per year and profit from sales in comparison with the original version - additional profit from sales and assessment of payback - increase in labor productivity, profitability of sales, operational leverage (level of production risk)
Saving current costs of the enterprise and reducing production costs	1. Development of project technology and its localization 2. The calculation of the reduction in the number of personnel, jobs, equipment and space, other cost elements for the enterprise as a whole during the implementation of the project 3. Calculation of project costs and reduction of current expenses of the enterprise 4. Determination of additional profit from the reduction of operating costs for the enterprise and the assessment of payback 5. Calculation of project-specific criteria-based performance indicators	- the number and current costs per year for the enterprise in comparison with the initial version - additional profit from sales and assessment of payback - increase in labor productivity, profitability of sales, operational leverage (level of production risk)

The main indicator of economic efficiency of projects of the personnel management system of any target orientation is the additional profit from sales. Its value depends on the relative reduction in the cost of sales and operational costs of the project. When implementing projects of the personnel management system aimed at increasing sales, the cost of production grows to a lesser extent than revenue. Formed "economies of scale" - the relative savings of constant costs of the company. The greater the share of fixed costs (respectively, the smaller the share of variable costs) in the cost of production of an enterprise, the greater the additional profit from sales in the implementation of such projects. It should be based on a ratio (1):

$$Rp = Rt * ds, \tag{1}$$

where Rp – the planned percentage of growth in sales volumes for the project; Rt – the estimated percentage growth in cost (current costs) for the project; ds – the share of variable costs in the cost of sales of the enterprise at the time of development of the business plan.

In this case, when planning the increase in sales as a result of the implementation of the personnel management system project by 1%, current costs (cost of sales) will increase with a share of variable costs in the cost of 0.8 by 0.8%, and with a share of variables costs 0.3, only 0.3%. The second situation (for an enterprise with a greater share of fixed costs) considers the calculation (2) with an additional increase in sales profit for an enterprise resulting in an annual sales volume of 150 million rubles per year will be 750 thousand rubles (0.5% of 150 million rubles will amount to 750 thousand Rubles).

$$0.8\% - 0.3\% = 0.5\% \tag{2}$$

Table 2. Economic indicators for evaluating a personnel management project

Economic indicators	Initial situation	Project №1	Project №2
Project objectives: saving current costs by reducing the number of		Reduction in managerial staff	Reduction of production staff
Number of employees	55	48	35
Investment in the project, mln. Rub.	–	0,01	0,01
Sales volume, million Rubles/year	190,000	190,000	190,000
Current expenses	160,000	158,8	158,0
	120,0	120,0	112,0
	40,0	38,8	46,0
(Cost), million Rubles/year	30.0	31,2	32,0
Including variables	–	1,2	2,0
Permanent profit from sales, million Rubles/year	–	Less than half a year	Less than half a year
Additional profit from sales million Rubles/year	287,9	329,9	452,4
Payback period, year	15,8	16,4	16,8
Productivity, (sales per person/month) thousand Rubles	2,33	2,24	2,44

To summarize the results of economic calculations and make decisions on the implementation of personnel management system projects, special comparative tables are recommended in the author's methodology. Table 2 combines the results of an economic analysis of two personnel management system projects aimed at reducing the number of personnel in a small industrial enterprise. The calculation results show that project №2 to reduce the number of production personnel requires an increase in fixed costs of the enterprise by 6 million rubles, but allows you to save 8 million rubles on variable costs of the enterprise. As a result, the planned additional profit from sales with constant sales volumes is 2 million rubles per year.

The implementation of project №1, despite the planned reduction in constant costs to 38.8 million, allows us to plan additional profit from sales of only 1.2 million rubles. in year. The implementation of project № 2 is also characterized by a significant increase in productivity from 287.9 to 452.4 thousand rubles. per person per month. But in this option, production risks increase: operating leverage increases from 2.33 to 2.44 million rubles.

For this enterprise, while working out a business development plan, the personnel management system project options aimed at increasing the volume of product sales were also considered. As can be seen from the table, this enterprise has a relatively high share of variable costs in the prime cost of 75% (120 out of 160 million rubles). As a result, the project version of personnel motivation aimed at increasing sales volumes by 0.6% allows us to plan additional profit from sales of only 420 thousand rubles. This is significantly less than the development options presented in Table 3 with the goal of reducing the number of staff (1.2 and 2.0 million rubles).

4   Discussion

With the main task of this research being creation of the mechanism effectively resolving organizations' everyday problems and avoiding the potential risks in a crisis, it should be taken into the account that the crises are rarely resolvable through the application of any predefined procedures and plans.

Future research could prove the new organizational paradigm of personnel management system projects enabling firms gain competitive advantages in an ever-changing world, where market globalization, empowerment, and information technology are becoming the most important.

5   Conclusion

The information received is sufficient to make an acceptable effective decision at the level of the enterprise's managers.

Thus, the presented methodology allows using relatively simple calculations to prepare material for decision-making by company executives.

The proposed methodology was developed and tested in the process of working with numerous crisis enterprises of small and medium-sized businesses in St. Petersburg and the Leningrad Region from the year 2003 to the year 2016. At the same time, for the financial and economic analysis, development of a strategy and business plans for resolving enterprises from the crisis, standard software products of the Voronov and Maximov consulting group were used: "Master of Finance: Analysis" and "Project Wizard: Budget Approach". When preparing materials for business planning, the monitoring model "Normative budget" was used, developed by the authors to expand the capabilities of standard software products. To apply the proposed methodology, it is also possible to use the standard software product "1C: Accounting 8.3" with significant improvements for each enterprise.

In 2014, the DR agricultural complex sharply reduced its efficiency: ROE fell to 11.3%. At the same time, the risk premium decreased to the level unacceptable to owners. Financial and economic analysis, formation of a development plan, investment and work with personnel plans, and its successful implementation allowed to significantly increase labor productivity and bring the ROE to 30.7%.

Tools should allow firms to accept the challenge of digitizing and be future directions of research. Reducing costs and time should allow companies to survive effectively. Firms may benefit from new information to better manage your resources and internal knowledge.

Acknowledgments. This research work was supported by the Academic Excellence Project 5-100 proposed by Peter the Great St. Petersburg Polytechnic University.

References

1. Akhmetshin, E.M., Ilyina, I.A., Kulibanova, V.V., Teor, T.R.: Employee engagement' management facilitates the recovery from crisis situations. In: Proceedings of the 2019 IEEE Communication Strategies in Digital Society Seminar, ComSDS 2019, St. Petersburg; Russian Federation, pp. 50–55 (2019). https://doi.org/10.1109/COMSDS.2019.8709645
2. Berens, V., Havranek, P.M.: Guidelines for Assessing the Effectiveness of Investments: Translate Engl., p. 496. Interexpert, Infra-M, Moscow (1995)
3. Boateng, P., Chen, Z., Ogunlana, S.O.: An analytical network process model for risks prioritisation in megaprojects. Int. J. Project Manage. 33(8), 1795–1811 (2015)
4. Boon, C., Eckardt, R., Lepak, D.P., Boselie, P.: Integrating strategic human capital and strategic human resource management. Int. J. Hum. Resour. Manage. **29**, 34–67 (2018). https://doi.org/10.1080/09585192.2017.1380063
5. Bril, A., Kalinina, O., Rasskazova, O.A.: Financial and economic aspects of the assessment of innovative projects in the human resource management system. In: Proceedings of the 31st International Business Information Management Association Conference, IBIMA 2018: Innovation Management and Education Excellence Through Vision 2020, pp. 5772–5782 (2019)
6. Bril, A.R., Kalinina, O.V., Ilin, I.V.: Economic analysis of projects in the improvement of the HR management system of enterprises. In: Proceedings of the 29th International Business Information Management Association Conference - Education Excellence and Innovation Management through Vision 2020: From Regional Development Sustainability to Global Economic Growth, pp. 2268–2277 (2017)
7. Bril, A., Kalinina, O., Kankovskaya, A., Vilken, V.: Operational risk management in financing environmental activities and personnel management projects. In: E3S Web of Conferences, vol. 110, p. 02018 (2019). www.e3s-conferences.org/10.1051/e3sconf/201911002018

8. Chen, M., Leung, V.C.M.: From cloud-based communications to cognition-based communications: a computing perspective. Comput. Commun. **128**, 74–79 (2018). https://doi.org/10.1016/j.comcom.2018.07.010
9. Dewasurendra, S., Judice, P., Zhu, Q.: Leveraging culture and leadership in crisis management. Eur. J. Training Dev. **43**(5–6), 554–569 (2019)
10. Dewasurendra, S., Judice, P., Zhu, Q.: The optimum leverage level of the banking sector. Risks **7**(2), 51 (2019)
11. e Silva, L.C., Costa, A.P.C.S.: Decision model for allocating human resources in information system projects. Int. J. Proj. Manag. 31, 100–108 (2013). https://doi.org/10.1016/j.ijproman.2012.06.008
12. Haneda, S., Ito, K.: Organizational and human resource management and innovation: which management practices are linked to product and/or process innovation? Res. Policy **47**(1), 194–208 (2018)
13. Kianto, A., Sáenz, J., Aramburu, N.: Knowledge-based human resource management practices, intellectual capital and innovation. J. Bus. Res. **81**, 11–20 (2017)
14. Koning De, L., Dongen Van, K., Thönissen, F., Essens, P., Vries De, T.: A tool to quickly increase knowledge for effective coordination in crises. In: Proceedings of the International ISCRAM Conference, 2017 May, Albi, France, pp. 220–233 (2017)
15. Lang, A., Pigneur, Y.: Digital trade of human competencies. In: Proceedings of the 32nd Hawaii International Conference on System Sciences (1999)
16. Lin, Y., Wang, X., Xu, R.: Semi-supervised human resource scheduling based on deep presentation in the cloud. EURASIP J. Wirel. Commun. Netw. **2020**(1), 1–9 (2020). https://doi.org/10.1186/s13638-020-01677-6
17. Luburić, R., Bhaduri, R.M.: A model of crisis prevention (based on managing change, quality management and risk management). J. Cent. Bank. Theory Pract. **8**(2), 33–49 (2019)
18. Nicholds, B.A., Mo, J.P.T.: Risk management of energy system for identifying optimal power mix with financial-cost minimization and environmental-impact mitigation under uncertainty. JMTM **29**(6), 1003 (2018)
19. Nizamidou, C., Vouzas, F., Gotzamani, K.: Exploring the interrelationship between quality, safety and HR within crisis management framework. TQM J. **31**(4), 541–562 (2019)
20. Oueida, S., Kotb, Y., Aloqaily, M., et al.: An edge computing based smart healthcare framework for resource management. Sensors (Switzerland) **18**, 1–22 (2018). https://doi.org/10.3390/s18124307
21. Rodionov, D., Rudskaia, I.: Problems of infrastructural development of "industry 4.0" in Russia on Sibur experience. In: Proceedings of the 32nd International Business Information Management Association Conference, pp. 3534–3544 (2018)
22. Saridakis, G., Lai, Y., Cooper, C.L.: Exploring the relationship between HRM and firm performance: a meta-analysis of longitudinal studies. Hum. Resour. Manage. Rev. **27**(1), 87–96 (2017)
23. Silver, N.: Finance, Society and Sustainability: How to Make the Financial System Work for the Economy, People and Planet. Palgrave Macmillan, London, p. 304 (2017)
24. Stojcic, N., Hashi, I., Orlic, E.: Creativity, innovation effectiveness and productive efficiency in the UK. Eur. J. Innov. Manage. **21**(4), 564–580 (2018). https://doi.org/10.1108/EJIM-11-2017-0166
25. Varma, T.: Understanding decision making during a crisis: an axiomatic model of cognitive decision choices. Int. J. Bus. Commun. **56**(2), 233–248 (2019)
26. Zhilenkova, E., Budanova, M., Bulkhov, N., Rodionov, D.: Reproduction of intellectual capital in innovative-digital economy environment. In: IOP Conference Series: Materials Science and Engineering, vol. 4971 (2019)
27. Zhou, Y., Li, H.: Asset diversification and systemic risk in the financial system. J. Econ. Interac. Coord. **14**(2), 247–272 (2017). https://doi.org/10.1007/s11403-017-0205-4

Author Index

Printed in the United States
By Bookmasters